CW00496849

ONE-POT PASTA

One-Pot
PASTA

65 Super Easy Recipes for One-and-Done Meals

Sarah Walker Caron

Photography by Darren Muir

ROCKRIDGE
PRESS

Copyright © 2019 by Rockridge Press, Emeryville, California

No part of this publication may be reproduced, stored in a retrieval system or transmitted in any form or by any means, electronic, mechanical, photocopying, recording, scanning or otherwise, except as permitted under Sections 107 or 108 of the 1976 United States Copyright Act, without the prior written permission of the Publisher. Requests to the Publisher for permission should be addressed to the Permissions Department, Rockridge Press, 6005 Shellmound Street, Suite 175, Emeryville, CA 94608.

Limit of Liability/Disclaimer of Warranty: The Publisher and the author make no representations or warranties with respect to the accuracy or completeness of the contents of this work and specifically disclaim all warranties, including without limitation warranties of fitness for a particular purpose. No warranty may be created or extended by sales or promotional materials. The advice and strategies contained herein may not be suitable for every situation. This work is sold with the understanding that the Publisher is not engaged in rendering medical, legal or other professional advice or services. If professional assistance is required, the services of a competent professional person should be sought. Neither the Publisher nor the author shall be liable for damages arising herefrom. The fact that an individual, organization or website is referred to in this work as a citation and/or potential source of further information does not mean that the author or the Publisher endorses the information the individual, organization or website may provide or recommendations they/it may make. Further, readers should be aware that websites listed in this work may have changed or disappeared between when this work was written and when it is read.

For general information on our other products and services or to obtain technical support, please contact our Customer Care Department within the United States at (866) 744-2665, or outside the United States at (510) 253-0500.

Rockridge Press publishes its books in a variety of electronic and print formats. Some content that appears in print may not be available in electronic books, and vice versa.

TRADEMARKS: Rockridge Press and the Rockridge Press logo are trademarks or registered trademarks of Callisto Media Inc. and/or its affiliates, in the United States and other countries, and may not be used without written permission. All other trademarks are the property of their respective owners. Rockridge Press is not associated with any product or vendor mentioned in this book.

Interior and Cover Designer: Suzanne LaGasa
Photo Art Director: Amy Hartmann
Editor: Kim Suarez
Production Editor: Andrew Yackira
Photography: Darren Muir

ISBN: Print 978-1-64152-330-1 |
eBook 978-1-64152-331-8

For Will and Paige—
may you always eat well.

Contents

Introduction

Long strands or curly shapes. Saucy or creamy. Robust with vegetables or tossed with seafood. There are many different ways to enjoy pasta. And it's a clear dinner favorite for busy folks all over because pasta is so easy to cook.

But what if it could be even easier?

One pot. One single pot. That's all you need to make the 50 recipes for pasta in this cookbook. From cheesy pastas to ones bursting with seafood, the recipes in this book will delight and satisfy many different eaters. But perhaps the best part of this collection of recipes is that many can be made with satisfying, hearty ingredients you probably already have in your kitchen.

It doesn't get much easier than that.

And that's what this cookbook is all about—easy and flavorful recipes for pastas that will make getting dinner on the table nearly effortless. Not only are they quick, but one-pot pastas are also efficient. Everything that goes into the pot adds to the flavor and complexity of the dish. You aren't pouring excess water down the drain or using multiple pots and pans to assemble these recipes. There's less to clean up, making the after-dinner chores easier, too.

To qualify as one-pot, these recipes were developed so that all of the cooking is done in just one pot or pan from start to finish. There's no draining of the cooking liquid or cooking done separately from that one pot. For this reason, you'll find two cooking methods in this book.

The first method is the All-in-One method, which calls for all the ingredients to be added to the pot at the same time. When the pasta is tender, in some recipes you might stir in herbs, cheese, or other flavor enhancers to finish it off, but that's it. These pastas are super easy and quick to make.

The second method is the Step-by-Step method, in which the dish is cooked in stages. For instance, there are a few chicken pastas where you sauté the chicken first then remove it from the pot while you cook the other ingredients. The chicken is then added back to the pot, along with other flavor enhancers, after the pasta has cooked to ensure that you don't overcook the chicken. These recipes may take a little longer with the added steps, but they are still pretty darn easy.

Of course, families cannot live by pasta alone. That's why the bonus chapter filled with additional recipes for salads and sides is so handy. These dishes were created for pairing with pastas and are great complements for the dishes in this book. My hope is not only that you try and love several of my recipes but also that once you see the process, you can venture out and create your own one-pot pasta dishes with your favorite mixture of ingredients by following the Make It Your Own chart (page 9) as well.

As a busy single mother to two kids in middle school, time is something I don't have a lot of. My children have sports practices, rehearsals, lessons, and homework filling their calendars and mine. I also have my full-time day job as an editor, my side hustle as the writer behind a food blog and freelance clients, and my work as a college instructor. My family and I know busy.

But we also make a point to have dinner together nearly every night. It's important time as a family, time where we catch up on our days and check in with one another. To make family dinners happen on busy nights, though, quick and easy recipes like the ones in this book are essential.

I hope you love the recipes in this book as much as my family does. Enjoy!

Chapter One

ONE-POT PASTA FUNDAMENTALS

You worked all day. The kids had practices and clubs and lessons. Everyone is finally arriving home, hungry and tired, asking "What's for dinner?"

Oh, that dreaded question.

But it doesn't have to be. With easy recipes for one-pot pastas, you can be armed with a cache of dinners that cook in minutes and satisfy even the pickiest of palates.

Grab a good pot with a tight-fitting lid, and let's get started.

THE FORMULA

This book includes 50 tried-and-true recipes for one-pot pastas. They are a great place to start. But if you want to try your own take on one-pot pasta, there's a pretty simple formula to follow.

If you have some or all of the following ingredients in your kitchen, you'll be able to start making your own one-pot pasta creations right away:

PASTA (8 OUNCES)

+

AROMATICS
(onions, garlic, etc.)

+

HERBS AND SPICES
(salt, pepper, oregano, basil, etc.)

+

LIQUID
(2¼ cups broth, stock, or water)

+

PROTEIN
(seafood, meat, sausage, beans, etc.)

+

VEGGIES
(tomatoes, bell peppers, carrots, etc.)

+

CHEESE
(mozzarella, Cheddar, etc.; optional)

+

TOPPINGS
(grated Parmesan, parsley, basil, etc.)

ONE-POT COOKING METHODS

What about technique? Not all one-pot pastas are made the same. In this book, there are two main cooking methods used: the All-in-One method, where all or most of the ingredients are combined in a pot and cooked together until the pasta is tender; and the Step-by-Step method, where ingredients are cooked in stages using the same pot. The All-in-One method is faster and less hands-on, while the Step-by-Step method allows for more nuanced flavor.

All-in-One Pasta

Gather your ingredients, cut and chop them as needed, and add them to the pot. Then cook, stirring occasionally. That's how easy the All-in-One pasta method is. This method can create some really flavorful pastas in a short amount of time.

METHOD

1. In a large pot or Dutch oven, combine all or most of the ingredients—be sure to read the directions thoroughly—and mix them together.

2. Cover the pot and bring the mixture to a boil over high heat. Reduce the heat to low and simmer, stirring occasionally, until the pasta is tender.

3. Remove the pot from the heat. Add any toppings or mix-ins and enjoy.

Step-by-Step Pasta

As the name suggests, Step-by-Step pasta is made using a few steps, allowing different ingredients to cook in the way that's best for them. Start by sautéing aromatics and/or proteins then remove the proteins from the pot. Like the All-in-One method, you then combine the remainder of the ingredients and cook until the pasta is tender. Add the protein and any other mix-ins to the pasta and you are ready to enjoy. This method allows for more flexibility and precision with the cooking since you aren't cooking everything at once, but it does take a little longer than the All-in-One method.

METHOD

1. In a large pot or Dutch oven, sauté the aromatics and/or protein. Remove the protein from the pot and set it aside.

2. Deglaze the pot with wine (optional).

3. Add the pasta, seasonings, and any veggies to the pot. Cover the pot and bring the mixture to a boil over high heat. Reduce the heat to low and simmer, stirring occasionally, until the pasta is tender.

4. Add the cooked protein and any mix-ins to the pot. Sprinkle with toppings and enjoy.

ALL-IN-ONE PASTA BEST PRACTICES

Before you get cooking, these tips will help you make great All-in-One pastas.

Mix up the liquids. Water's fine, but when making All-in-One pasta, the liquid becomes part of the flavor. Don't be afraid to use broth, wine, juice, milk, and more to create a fragrant, flavorful pasta.

Don't over-season. You can always add more salt, pepper, and other seasonings, but you can't go back once these ingredients are already in the pot. Use salt especially sparingly.

If your pasta is water-based, add oil. A tablespoon of oil will help prevent the pasta noodles from sticking together.

Don't forget to stir. Stirring is essential to prevent sticking. Stir at least three times while the pasta is cooking.

If you forget to stir, don't panic. Let the pasta cool down for a few minutes and those stuck-on bits will magically become less stuck.

If the liquid evaporates before the cooking time is over, add water. Depending on the pot you're using, sometimes evaporation will leave the pot dry. Simply add water to help keep the pasta cooking. I usually add ½ to 1 cup at a time.

STEP-BY-STEP PASTA BEST PRACTICES

Prepare your ingredients before you start cooking. Have your herbs and vegetables chopped, your proteins cut to the right sizes, and your liquids measured. This will make the process of preparing the dish much easier.

Don't forget to remove the protein. The name of the game here is to not overcook. Even cooked in liquid, chicken can dry out and shrimp can turn rubbery.

Use salt sparingly. Especially when using flavorful broths. No one wants over-salted food.

Have a bowl ready. When it's time to transfer the protein, a bowl makes the process much easier.

Know that you don't always have to remove the protein. Ground meats and sausage can actually be enhanced by cooking in the liquid.

INGREDIENTS

When cooking, it's the ingredients that matter most. Good-quality ingredients, cooked well, make good food. Shop your local farmers' markets, buy fresh in-season produce, and spring for the better-quality chicken stock. Your taste buds will thank you.

Pasta

Secret number one: I almost always buy store-brand pasta. Secret number two: Store-brand pasta is usually name-brand pasta in generic packaging. I am reasonably certain that my favorite name-brand pasta maker manufactures the store brand I buy.

It doesn't matter how much you pay for pasta. What does matter is how it cooks and its quality.

And when it comes to one-pot pastas, nearly any pasta variety will work—as long as it's not a pasta marketed as quick-cooking. Those varieties will overcook.

Here are some of my favorite pastas to use in one-pot pastas:

- Spaghetti
- Linguine
- Fettuccine
- Ziti
- Penne
- Rigatoni
- Farfalle
- Medium shells
- Elbow macaroni
- Orzo
- Rotini
- Orecchiette
- Cavatappi
- Gemelli
- Campanelle

You can also use angel hair, thin spaghetti, and vermicelli, but these will cook faster than other pastas. For best results, be sure to watch closely for doneness or follow a recipe intended for these pastas. Two more great options are tortellini and ravioli.

Aromatics

With distinctive smells and flavors, aromatics help shape the flavor of the pasta. But how you cook them (or don't cook them) will determine what flavor they impart. Pungent garlic, for instance, can be used in small quantities raw to add a zest to dishes. The flavor is boldest when raw. When sautéed, garlic retains some of that zest but mellows enough not to have a sharp bite. When boiled, the flavor is mild but earthy.

In addition to garlic, other aromatics commonly used include onions, shallots, leeks, ginger, carrots, and celery.

Herbs and Spices

Herbs and spices are important to the overall flavor of one-pot pastas (and many other dishes). They boost and shift the flavor.

Here are some herbs and spices to keep on hand:

- Dried basil
- Dried oregano
- Dried thyme
- Dried rosemary
- Paprika
- Ground cumin
- Garlic powder
- Ground cinnamon
- Freshly ground black pepper
- Salt

Liquids

The liquid that the pasta cooks in will influence its flavor. Chicken broth has a mild flavor that gives pasta a subtle richness. Chicken stock has a similar impact. Vegetable broth imparts whatever flavors the broth is based on, so be sure to choose one with a base flavor you like. Water, on the other hand, won't alter the flavor, which sometimes is just right for a dish.

Adding these milder liquids as the base and smaller amounts of bold liquids like soy sauce, lemon juice, or heavy cream can prevent those flavorful liquids from becoming overwhelming.

Proteins

Although proteins aren't required for every pasta, they can add good bulk to a dish. Commonly used proteins include ground beef, turkey or chicken, sausage, shrimp, clams, steak, beans, and tofu.

SPICE BLENDS

The following spice blends can be made in advance and stored in an airtight container in the cupboard. Use a few teaspoons in pastas.

Italian Spice Blend: Equal parts dried basil, dried oregano, dried rosemary, and dried thyme. Garlic powder can also be added. This is good in tomato-based pasta sauces.

Greek Spice Blend: Equal parts dried basil, dried oregano, garlic powder, and paprika with a half part ground cinnamon. Use this in vinaigrettes.

Mexican Spice Blend: Equal parts ground cumin, salt, paprika, garlic powder, and a half part dried oregano with a double amount of chili powder. This can be used with meats such as ground beef, ground chicken, and ground turkey. Add water to it to form a sauce.

Preparation of proteins varies from dish to dish; however, generally it's best to cook ground beef, steak, chicken, and seafood before cooking the pasta. Reserve the proteins, once cooked, and stir them into the pasta once it's complete. Also, large pieces of chicken, beef, and other proteins should be cut into uniform, bite-size pieces so that they cook evenly.

Veggies

Some good vegetables to have on hand as staples in your kitchen for making one-pot pastas include the following:

- Bell peppers
- Carrots
- Green beans
- Onions
- Peas (frozen)
- Shallots
- Sweet potatoes
- Tomatoes

The following vegetables are also frequently used in recipes in this book and are great for bulking up pasta dishes with extra nutrients and flavors:

- Asparagus
- Beet greens
- Cauliflower
- Eggplant
- Leeks
- Napa cabbage
- Spinach

When prepping veggies, dicing is typically the best method. This works for both All-in-One and Step-by-Step pasta recipes. (Note that you'll want to chop leafy greens, however.)

Cheeses

Cheese can enhance the flavor of some dishes. Some common cheeses used in pasta dishes include the following:

- Mozzarella
- Cheddar
- Parmesan
- Romano
- Feta
- Brie
- Gouda
- Asiago
- Blue cheese

Cheeses are usually either grated or crumbled, depending on the type of cheese (semisoft cheeses like blue cheese and feta are crumbled; hard cheeses like Gouda, Romano, and Cheddar are grated). A few cheeses, such as fresh mozzarella and Brie, are best used diced.

Many times, it's best to add the cheese at the end of the cooking time. This way, you won't have to worry about it sticking or burning.

Toppings

Toppings can add crunch, brightness, and other flavors to a pasta. Here are a few good ones to consider:

- Bread crumbs
- Chopped fresh herbs
- Chopped microgreens
- Chopped nuts
- Chopped onions
- Crumbled bacon
- Crumbled crackers
- Hot sauce

TOOLS AND EQUIPMENT

The Pot

Now, what should you cook your pasta in? Not just any pot will do.

The ideal pot will heat evenly; be nonstick; hold a lot of pasta, liquid, and mix-ins; and have a tight-fitting lid. My preferred pot is a cast iron Dutch oven, and that is what I reach for most often. I also have a nonstick pot that I like, but the lid does not fit tightly, so pastas made in it need more watching when they cook. For some recipes, especially those involving cheese, a nonstick pot will be essential to prevent sticking and burning of the cheese. For all the other recipes, any type of large, heavy-bottomed pot or Dutch oven with a tight-fitting lid will work great.

Other Pasta-Cooking Essentials

To make the recipes in the book, I recommend having the following kitchen tools handy:

- Cheese grater
- Cutting board
- Handheld juicer
- Chef's knife
- Kitchen scale
- Measuring cups and spoons
- Pot holders
- Small, medium, and large mixing bowls
- Vegetable peeler
- Wooden spatulas

MAKE IT YOUR OWN

Recipes in this book will do the work for you when it comes to building the perfect pasta for dinner, but for days when you don't have all the ingredients to follow a recipe, here are some easy options to mix and match with the formula (page 2) to make it simple for you to bring together whatever you have lying around in your fridge.

PASTA (8 OUNCES)	AROMATICS	HERBS AND SPICES	LIQUID (2¼ CUPS)	PROTEIN	VEGGIES	TOPPINGS
Elbow macaroni	Onion	Salt	Broth	Steak	Cherry tomatoes	Grated Parmesan
Rotini	Garlic	Black pepper	Stock	Pork	Zucchini	Chopped parsley
Penne	Shallots	Oregano	Water	Shrimp	Corn	Toasted bread crumbs
Farfalle	Leeks	Basil	Beer	Pancetta	Broccoli	
Spaghetti	Scallions	Rosemary	Wine	Bacon	Eggplant	Fried onions
Angel hair	Ginger	Thyme	Juice	Chicken breast	Sweet bell peppers	Sliced avocado
Fettuccine				Black beans	Roasted red bell peppers	Thinly sliced basil
Linguine				Cannellini beans		
Shells				Chickpeas		Chopped cilantro

Chapter Two

CHEESE PASTAS

Left: Creamy Gorgonzola Fettuccine with Broccoli, page 19

CHEESY SPINACH-ARTICHOKE PASTA

SERVES 4

PREP TIME: 5 MINUTES | COOK TIME: 30 MINUTES

ALL-IN-ONE, QUICK PREP

This saucy pasta tastes like the beloved spinach-artichoke dip that's an appetizer staple at so many restaurants and on so many party tables. Although this calls for fresh baby spinach, frozen chopped spinach can be substituted in a pinch without seriously affecting the flavor. Serve this with a tossed salad or crusty bread.

8 ounces dry penne

2 cups chicken stock

1 (14-ounce) can quartered artichoke hearts, drained and roughly chopped

½ cup white wine

2 garlic cloves, minced

1 teaspoon dried basil

1 teaspoon dried thyme

1 teaspoon salt

3 cups fresh baby spinach

½ cup heavy cream

½ cup shredded mozzarella cheese

½ cup freshly grated Parmesan cheese

1. In a large pot or Dutch oven, combine the penne, chicken stock, artichoke hearts, wine, garlic, basil, thyme, and salt.

2. Cover the pot and bring the mixture to a boil over medium-high heat. Reduce the heat to medium-low and simmer, covered, for 12 to 15 minutes, stirring occasionally, until the pasta is tender.

3. Stir in the baby spinach, heavy cream, mozzarella cheese, and Parmesan cheese. Cover the pot and continue cooking until the sauce begins to thicken, about 3 to 4 minutes. Remove the pot from the heat and let the pasta sit for 5 minutes before serving.

SUBSTITUTION TIP: This pasta can be vegetarian if you swap the chicken stock for half vegetable stock and half water. Be sure to choose a vegetable stock with a base flavor you like (I prefer an onion-based one).

CREAMY SPICY PARMESAN AND RED PEPPER FETTUCCINE

SERVES 4
PREP TIME: 10 MINUTES | COOK TIME: 20 MINUTES
ALL-IN-ONE, 30 MINUTES

In Maine, where I live, winters are long and particularly cold. On the coldest days, warm, creamy pastas are a delight. This one—creamy, bright, and a little spicy—is perfect for days like that (or whenever you feel like a warm cheesy pasta). This comfort food with a twist is a flavorful alternative to fettuccine alfredo. Also, don't be afraid to change up the cheese in this: Romano or Asiago cheese can be used in place of the Parmesan, if desired.

8 ounces dry fettuccine
1½ cups chicken stock
3 roasted red bell peppers, diced
1 small onion, diced
½ cup white wine
2 garlic cloves, minced
1 teaspoon kosher salt
½ teaspoon red pepper flakes
½ teaspoon dried thyme
½ cup heavy cream
1 cup freshly grated Parmesan cheese

1. In a large pot or Dutch oven, combine the fettuccine, chicken stock, bell peppers, onion, wine, garlic, salt, red pepper flakes, and thyme. Stir.

2. Cover the pot and bring the mixture to a boil over medium-high heat. Reduce the heat to low and simmer for 10 to 12 minutes, until the fettucine is tender, stirring several times while cooking.

3. Remove the pot from the heat. Stir in the heavy cream and Parmesan cheese.

4. Taste and season with additional salt and black pepper as needed.

OPTION TIP: Jarred roasted red bell peppers work great in this recipe, but if you want to roast your own it's easy. Preheat the oven to 425°F. Place the peppers on a baking sheet lined with aluminum foil and roast them for 20 to 25 minutes, turning once or twice, until the skin is loose and charred. Remove the peppers from the oven, let them cool, remove the skin and seeds, and use as desired.

MACARONI AND CHEESE

SERVES 4

PREP TIME: 5 MINUTES | COOK TIME: 25 MINUTES

ALL-IN-ONE, 30 MINUTES, QUICK PREP, VEGETARIAN

When it comes to comfort food, macaroni and cheese is the ultimate—for those of us who love cheese, that is. But what if you could make a homemade version that's better than the familiar and ubiquitous box? You can! This rich and creamy recipe is ready in about 30 minutes. It will quickly become a favorite. For a well-rounded meal, serve this with a protein like roasted chicken or pork chops and a salad.

8 ounces dry elbow macaroni
1¼ cups milk
1 cup water
1 cup shredded Cheddar cheese
½ teaspoon salt
½ teaspoon ground mustard
2 tablespoons heavy cream (optional)

1. In a large nonstick pot or Dutch oven, combine the macaroni, milk, water, Cheddar cheese, salt, and mustard.

2. Cover the pot and bring the mixture to a boil over medium-high heat, stirring once or twice. Reduce the heat to low and cook for 10 to 12 minutes, stirring frequently, until the pasta is tender.

3. Remove the pot from the heat. Stir in the heavy cream and Parmesan cheese.

4. Taste and season with additional salt and black pepper as needed.

RECIPE TIP: Cheddar is my favorite cheese in this dish, but it's tasty with other cheeses like Gouda, Monterey Jack, pepper Jack, or a combination of several.

TOMATO-BRIE FETTUCCINE

The combination of tomatoes and Brie cheese with warm pasta takes me back to high school. My mom made a pasta with those flavors, and it was a revelation—creamy, bright, and absolutely delicious. This easy version is a satisfying treat.

8 ounces dry fettuccine
8 ounces Brie cheese, cubed
2 cups diced fresh tomatoes
2 cups water
¼ cup white wine
2 garlic cloves, thinly sliced
1 tablespoon extra-virgin olive oil
1 teaspoon dried basil
Salt
Freshly ground black pepper

1. In a large nonstick pot or Dutch oven, combine the fettuccine, Brie cheese, tomatoes, water, wine, garlic, olive oil, and basil.

2. Cover the pot and bring the mixture to a boil over medium heat. Reduce the heat to low and simmer for 8 to 10 minutes, stirring occasionally, until the pasta is tender.

3. Season with salt and black pepper.

INGREDIENT TIP: If you freeze the Brie for 5 to 10 minutes, it's easier to cube. Also, for the creamiest pasta, remove the rind.

CHEESY BUFFALO CHICKEN MACARONI

SERVES 4

PREP TIME: 10 MINUTES | COOK TIME: 30 MINUTES

STEP-BY-STEP

Calling all Buffalo chicken lovers! Creamy, spicy, and hearty, this satisfying version of macaroni and cheese is delightful on cold days (or anytime you're craving the classic combination of Buffalo sauce, chicken, and Cheddar cheese sauce).

1 pound skinless, boneless chicken breast, cut into 1-inch pieces
2 tablespoons dried bread crumbs
1 teaspoon cornstarch
2 tablespoons extra-virgin olive oil
8 ounces dry elbow macaroni or small shells
1¼ cups milk
1 cup water
1 cup shredded Cheddar cheese
½ teaspoon ground mustard
½ teaspoon salt
¼ cup Buffalo sauce
¼ cup crumbled blue cheese (optional)
1 celery stalk, coarsely chopped (optional)

1. In a medium bowl, combine the chicken, bread crumbs, and cornstarch.

2. In a large nonstick pot or Dutch oven, heat the olive oil over medium heat. Add the chicken, discarding any excess bread crumbs. Cook, stirring often, until the chicken is browned and cooked through, about 8 to 10 minutes. Transfer the chicken to another medium bowl.

3. In the same pot, combine the macaroni, milk, water, Cheddar cheese, mustard, and salt.

4. Cover the pot and bring the mixture to a boil over medium-high heat. Reduce the heat to low and simmer for 10 to 12 minutes, stirring frequently, until the pasta is tender. Remove the pot from the heat.

5. Stir in the chicken and Buffalo sauce. Let the pasta sit for 5 minutes.

6. Serve with a sprinkling of crumbled blue cheese (if using) and chopped celery (if using).

OPTION TIP: For an even spicier experience, drizzle the pasta with additional Buffalo sauce before serving.

BEER CHEESE PENNE WITH TOMATOES

SERVES 4

PREP TIME: 5 MINUTES | COOK TIME: 20 MINUTES

ALL-IN-ONE, 30 MINUTES, QUICK PREP, VEGETARIAN

This is the ultimate game day pasta. And the best part? The beer you choose will completely alter the flavor of this pasta. Feeling like something hoppier? Choose an IPA. Something richer? Try a stout. I usually opt for an American lager, which has a subtler flavor.

8 ounces dry penne

1¼ cups milk

1 cup beer

1 cup shredded aged Gouda cheese

1 cup halved cherry tomatoes

1 shallot, quartered and thinly sliced

½ teaspoon salt

½ teaspoon ground mustard

1. In a large nonstick pot or Dutch oven, combine the penne, milk, beer, Gouda cheese, tomatoes, shallot, salt, and mustard.

2. Cover the pot and bring the mixture to a boil over medium-high heat. Reduce the heat to low and simmer for 10 to 12 minutes, stirring frequently, until the pasta is tender.

3. Let the pasta sit for 5 minutes before serving.

INGREDIENT TIP: Use a wider grating tool for the cheese for best results. This will create larger shreds that slowly melt into the sauce.

CHEESY STOVETOP ZITI

SERVES 4

PREP TIME: 5 MINUTES | COOK TIME: 30 MINUTES

STEP-BY-STEP, VEGETARIAN, QUICK PREP

When I was first learning to cook, baked ziti was a favorite. It's a simple, comforting combination of ziti, marinara sauce, ricotta cheese, and mozzarella cheese that's pretty straightforward to assemble. This version, though, makes it even easier with a from-scratch sauce that cooks with the pasta and a simple stovetop finish. The key is to only stir this just enough to incorporate the ricotta into the recipe without actually mixing it in.

1 (28-ounce) can crushed tomatoes
8 ounces dry ziti
2 cups water
3 garlic cloves, minced
1 teaspoon dried basil
1 teaspoon dried oregano
1 teaspoon salt
1 dried bay leaf
½ cup ricotta cheese
1 cup shredded mozzarella cheese

1. In a large pot or Dutch oven, combine the crushed tomatoes, ziti, water, garlic, basil, oregano, salt, and bay leaf.

2. Cover the pot and bring the mixture to a boil over high heat. Reduce the heat to low and cook for 10 to 12 minutes, until the pasta is tender and most of the liquid has evaporated, stirring every 3 to 4 minutes. Uncover the pot and taste the pasta. Adjust the seasonings as desired.

3. Dollop the ricotta cheese into the pot and stir gently to distribute it throughout the pasta. Sprinkle with the mozzarella cheese.

4. Cover the pot and cook for an additional 2 to 3 minutes, until the mozzarella is melted.

5. Uncover the pot, remove it from the heat, and let the pasta sit for 5 minutes before serving.

OPTION TIP: If you are using a Dutch oven, this recipe can be finished off in a 375°F oven. Bake it for 5 to 7 minutes, until the cheese is melty and browned in spots.

CREAMY GORGONZOLA FETTUCCINE WITH BROCCOLI

SERVES 4

PREP TIME: 10 MINUTES | COOK TIME: 20 MINUTES

ALL-IN-ONE, 30 MINUTES

When I was a little girl, my uncle Hugo convinced me to eat broccoli and cauliflower by making me a homemade cheese sauce to pour over them. Whenever I have dishes that combine either of those vegetables with a creamy, cheesy sauce, I think of him. This pasta is no exception, and it's also one of my daughter's favorite dishes in this book. It's loaded with Gorgonzola cheese, which bathes the pasta and broccoli. I think Hugo would approve.

4 cups roughly chopped fresh broccoli
    (including stems)
8 ounces dry fettuccine
1½ cups water
½ cup chicken stock
3 garlic cloves, minced
1 shallot, roughly chopped
1 teaspoon dried rosemary
1 teaspoon kosher salt
½ cup heavy cream
½ cup crumbled Gorgonzola cheese
Freshly ground black pepper

TIME-SAVING TIP: Frozen broccoli florets can be substituted for fresh broccoli. Do not defrost them before adding them to the pot.

1. In a large nonstick pot or Dutch oven, combine the broccoli, fettuccine, water, chicken stock, garlic, shallot, rosemary, and salt.

2. Cover the pot and bring the mixture to a boil over medium-high heat. Reduce the heat to low and simmer for 10 to 12 minutes, stirring occasionally, until the pasta is tender.

3. Remove the pot from the heat. Stir in the heavy cream and Gorgonzola cheese.

4. Taste and season with black pepper and additional salt as needed.

SPINACH-FETA SHELLS

SERVES 4

PREP TIME: 10 MINUTES | COOK TIME: 20 MINUTES

ALL-IN-ONE, 30 MINUTES, VEGETARIAN

Bert and Ernie. Abbott and Costello. Spinach and feta. Some things just go together. Reminiscent of a pasta salad I used to purchase at the grocery store, this dish is excellent hot or cold. Leftovers make excellent lunches.

8 ounces dry medium shells

2 cups water

2 cups fresh baby spinach

2 garlic cloves, minced

1 teaspoon salt

½ teaspoon freshly ground black pepper

½ cup crumbled feta cheese

2 tablespoons finely chopped fresh parsley

1 tablespoon freshly squeezed lemon juice

1. In a large pot or Dutch oven, combine the shells, water, baby spinach, garlic, salt, and black pepper.

2. Cover the pot and bring the mixture to a boil over medium heat. Reduce the heat to low. Simmer for 10 to 12 minutes, stirring occasionally, until the pasta is tender.

3. Remove the pot from the heat and stir in the feta cheese, parsley, and lemon juice. Taste and adjust the seasonings as desired.

SUBSTITUTION TIP: For lemony flavor without acidity, substitute the zest of 1 lemon for the lemon juice.

BLUE CHEESE, BRUSSELS SPROUTS, AND RED ONION FARFALLE

SERVES 4

PREP TIME: 15 MINUTES | COOK TIME: 30 MINUTES

STEP-BY-STEP, VEGETARIAN

The process of sautéing brings out the natural sweetness in red onions and Brussels sprouts. These veggies are then cooked with pasta, garlic, and a little balsamic vinegar for a rich sauce. The blue cheese stirred in at the end has a bold sharpness that contrasts nicely with the other flavors.

2 tablespoons extra-virgin olive oil

3 cups trimmed and thinly sliced Brussels sprouts

1 large red onion, quartered and thinly sliced

Salt

Freshly ground black pepper

8 ounces dry farfalle

2 cups water

1 garlic clove, minced

2 tablespoons balsamic vinegar

½ cup crumbled blue cheese

1. In a large pot or Dutch oven, heat the olive oil over medium heat. Add the Brussels sprouts and onion, and season with salt and black pepper. Cook, stirring, until the vegetables have softened and are beginning to brown, about 8 to 10 minutes.

2. Add the farfalle, water, garlic, balsamic vinegar, and 1 teaspoon salt. Cover the pot and bring the mixture to a boil. Reduce the heat to low and simmer, stirring occasionally, until the pasta is tender, about 12 to 14 minutes.

3. Remove the pot from the heat and stir in the blue cheese.

TIME-SAVING TIP: Many grocery stores carry presliced Brussels sprouts in the produce section. That option can make quick work of preparing this recipe.

GARLIC-PARSLEY PARMESAN PASTA

SERVES 4

PREP TIME: 5 MINUTES | COOK TIME: 15 MINUTES

ALL-IN-ONE, 30 MINUTES, QUICK PREP, VEGETARIAN

What happens when you sauté garlic in olive oil, then add the pasta and just enough water to cook it in the pot? You get a perfectly cooked, garlicky pasta without using a ton of olive oil. Now, what happens when you stir in chopped parsley and freshly grated Parmesan cheese? You get the creamiest Parmesan pasta without cream ever.

2 tablespoons extra-virgin olive oil

4 garlic cloves, minced

8 ounces dry vermicelli

2¼ cups water

1 teaspoon salt

⅓ cup finely chopped fresh parsley

1 cup freshly grated Parmesan cheese

SUBSTITUTION TIP: Any hard cheese can be substituted for the Parmesan in this recipe. It will alter the flavor though. Romano, for instance, will make for a sharper flavor, while an herbed Asiago will make this dish more fragrant.

1. In a large pot or Dutch oven, heat the olive oil over medium heat. Add the garlic and cook until fragrant, about 1 to 2 minutes. Do not let it brown.

2. Add the vermicelli, water, and salt to the pot. Cover the pot and bring the mixture to a boil over high heat. Reduce the heat to low and simmer for 8 to 10 minutes, stirring occasionally, until the pasta is tender. Remove the pot from the heat and stir in the parsley and Parmesan cheese.

CREAMY ASIAGO-TOMATO RIGATONI

SERVES 4

PREP TIME: 5 MINUTES | COOK TIME: 20 MINUTES

ALL-IN-ONE, 30 MINUTES, QUICK PREP, VEGETARIAN

With a flavor reminiscent of vodka sauce (but without the vodka, of course), this saucy pasta dish has a pleasant, creamy flavor and is dotted with bits of tomato. Try serving it alongside a pot roast or a breaded chicken breast. It's also good with a salad.

8 ounces dry rigatoni

2 cups water

1 (15.5-ounce) can diced tomatoes, undrained

2 garlic cloves, minced

1 teaspoon salt

½ teaspoon dried oregano

½ teaspoon dried basil

1 cup freshly grated Asiago cheese

½ cup heavy cream

OPTION TIP: Finishing this recipe off with fresh herbs can add a nice dimension to the dish. Try sprinkling it with chopped fresh parsley or basil.

1. In a large pot or Dutch oven, combine the rigatoni, water, tomatoes, garlic, salt, oregano, and basil. Cover the pot and bring the mixture to a boil over high heat. Reduce the heat to low and cook for 10 to 12 minutes, stirring occasionally, until the pasta is tender. Remove the pot from the heat.

2. Stir in the Asiago cheese and heavy cream. Taste and adjust the seasonings as desired.

Chapter Three

VEGGIE PASTAS

Left: Fragrant Sweet Potato and Red Onion Shells, page 35

TOMATO-BASIL ANGEL HAIR

SERVES 4
PREP TIME: 15 MINUTES | COOK TIME: 20 MINUTES
ALL-IN-ONE, 30 MINUTES, VEGAN

Fresh and fragrant, this easy pasta is lovely in summertime when tomatoes and basil are ripe. But it can also be a comforting reminder of warm summer days in the dark, cold winter months. Any small, fresh tomato will work. Try this dish with grape tomatoes, yellow tomatoes, or multihued ones from your tomato plants.

8 ounces dry angel hair
1 pint cherry tomatoes, halved
2 shallots, halved and thinly sliced
½ cup thinly sliced fresh basil, divided
2 garlic cloves, minced
½ teaspoon salt
2 cups water

1. In a large pot or Dutch oven, combine the angel hair (break it in half to fit, if needed), tomatoes, shallots, ¼ cup of the basil, garlic, salt, and water.

2. Cover the pot and bring the mixture to a boil over medium heat. Reduce the heat to low and simmer for 10 to 12 minutes, stirring occasionally, until the pasta is tender.

3. Uncover the pot and stir. Taste and adjust the seasonings as desired. Sprinkle with the remaining ¼ cup basil just before serving.

OPTION TIP: What's better than tomato-basil pasta? Tomato-basil pasta with fresh mozzarella! While it won't be vegan, stirring in ½ cup diced fresh mozzarella just before serving is pretty tasty.

SAUCY SPAGHETTI MARINARA

SERVES 4

PREP TIME: 5 MINUTES | COOK TIME: 20 MINUTES

ALL-IN-ONE, 30 MINUTES, QUICK PREP, VEGAN

Seasoned with garlic, basil, and oregano, this easy spaghetti is coated with a rich marinara. It reminds me of family dinners as a child. A saucy pasta, this is excellent served with crusty, warm Garlic Bread (page 85).

1 (28-ounce) can crushed tomatoes
8 ounces dry spaghetti
2 cups water
3 garlic cloves, minced
1 teaspoon dried basil
1 teaspoon dried oregano
1 teaspoon salt
1 dried bay leaf

OPTION TIP: This sauce will thicken upon standing, so resting it for a few minutes before serving is a good idea. And while many people prefer to take the bay leaf out of food before serving, my grandmother taught me to leave it in. Whoever gets the bay leaf in their dish gets an extra dose of luck—or so the story goes. (Just be sure not to eat it!)

1. In a large pot or Dutch oven, combine the crushed tomatoes, spaghetti (break it in half to fit, if needed), water, garlic, basil, oregano, salt, and bay leaf.

2. Cover the pot and bring the mixture to a boil. Reduce the heat to low and cook for 8 to 10 minutes, stirring every 2 to 3 minutes, until the pasta is tender and most of the liquid has evaporated.

3. Uncover the pot and cook for an additional 2 to 3 minutes, until the sauce thickens slightly.

4. Stir well. Taste and adjust the seasonings as desired.

SESAME NOODLES WITH VEGGIES

SERVES 4

PREP TIME: 20 MINUTES | COOK TIME: 15 MINUTES

ALL-IN-ONE, VEGAN

When I first moved to Manhattan in 1998, I was wowed by all the convenience dishes I could pick up at markets around the city. I tried tabbouleh, smoked fresh mozzarella, and so much more. I also tried sesame noodles for the first time, and they were unlike anything I'd had before. This recipe is my version of those noodles, with the addition of lots of veggies. Tossed with a savory, nutty, slightly sweet peanut sauce and sesame seeds, this pasta is divine served hot, warm, or cold. Try it with grilled chicken on the side.

8 ounces dry thin spaghetti

1 cup finely shredded napa cabbage

1 medium orange or red bell pepper, thinly sliced

½ cup shredded carrots

1½ cups water

¼ cup soy sauce

¼ cup rice vinegar

¼ cup peanut butter

2 tablespoons light brown sugar

1 tablespoon peeled and minced fresh ginger

2 tablespoons toasted sesame oil

1 teaspoon sesame seeds

1. In a large pot or Dutch oven, stir together the spaghetti, napa cabbage, bell pepper, carrots, water, soy sauce, rice vinegar, peanut butter, brown sugar, and ginger.

2. Cover the pot and bring the mixture to a boil over medium-high heat. Reduce the heat to low and simmer for 8 to 10 minutes, stirring occasionally, until the pasta is tender.

3. Remove the pot from the heat and stir in the sesame oil and sesame seeds.

TIME-SAVING TIP: This pasta makes great lunches. Make a batch and divide it into containers for easy grabbing. Store the pasta in the refrigerator for up to 5 days.

LEMON-GARLIC CAULIFLOWER ZITI

SERVES 4
PREP TIME: 10 MINUTES | COOK TIME: 20 MINUTES
ALL-IN-ONE, 30 MINUTES

My family cannot get enough cauliflower. Roasted, sautéed, chopped, steamed—no matter how I prepare it, they devour it. This pasta is no exception. They even fight over the lemony, garlicky leftovers. Although this calls for dried thyme, you could also use fresh minced thyme, but be sure to use about double the amount for the same flavor.

1 small head cauliflower, cut into
    1-inch pieces
8 ounces dry ziti
2 cups chicken broth
3 garlic cloves, minced
1 lemon, juiced and zested
1 teaspoon dried thyme
1 teaspoon salt

TIME-SAVING TIP: Frozen cauliflower can be substituted, if desired. Do not defrost it.

1. In a large pot or Dutch oven, combine the cauliflower, ziti, chicken broth, garlic, lemon juice and zest, thyme, and salt.

2. Cover the pot and bring the mixture to a boil over medium-high heat. Reduce the heat to low and simmer for 12 to 14 minutes, stirring occasionally, until the pasta and cauliflower are tender.

3. Remove the pot from the heat. Taste and adjust the seasonings as desired.

GARLIC AND WHITE BEAN PASTA WITH SPINACH

SERVES 4 TO 6

PREP TIME: 15 MINUTES | COOK TIME: 20 MINUTES

ALL-IN-ONE, VEGAN

In high school, I gave up meat and became a vegetarian. To my parents' credit, they just went with it and also ate less meat. To keep things interesting, they would try whatever vegetarian recipes they could, including several pasta dishes with beans in them. As I was working on this recipe, I was reminded of that time and how much I loved cannellini beans. This hearty pasta is filled with meaty white beans and fragrant garlic, and is finished off with bright, fresh spinach.

1 (15.5-ounce) can white beans, rinsed and drained
12 ounces dry cavatappi
3½ cups vegetable stock
4 garlic cloves, thinly sliced
2 cups fresh baby spinach
Salt
Freshly ground black pepper

SUBSTITUTION TIP: Other greens can be used in this recipe as well. For instance, chopped Swiss chard or beet greens are delightful with this. Add them when there is about 3 minutes left to the cooking time so they soften a bit.

1. In a large pot or Dutch oven, combine the beans, cavatappi, vegetable stock, and garlic.

2. Cover the pot and bring the mixture to a boil over medium heat. Stir, reduce the heat to low, and simmer for 10 to 12 minutes, stirring occasionally, until the pasta is tender.

3. Remove the pot from the heat and stir in the baby spinach. Allow the pasta to sit for 5 minutes and stir again.

4. Taste and season with salt and black pepper.

ROTINI WITH LEEKS, TOMATOES, AND PEAS

SERVES 4

PREP TIME: 15 MINUTES | COOK TIME: 30 MINUTES

ALL-IN-ONE, VEGAN

Sweet leeks, juicy tomatoes, and bright peas—this vegetable-filled pasta dish is bursting with flavors. This is best served in late summer when you can get most of these veggies fresh from the farmers' market. And if you can find fresh peas, go for it. Be sure to cook them first before adding them to the pasta.

8 ounces dry rotini

2¼ cups water

2 leeks, rinsed, halved, and white and light green parts cut into ¼-inch-thick slices

1 pint grape or cherry tomatoes, halved

1 cup frozen peas

1 teaspoon dried basil

1 teaspoon salt

INGREDIENT TIP: Diced tomatoes can be substituted for the grape or cherry tomatoes. Choose a larger variety, not a paste (e.g., Roma or plum) tomato.

1. In a large pot or Dutch oven, combine the rotini, water, leeks, tomatoes, peas, basil, and salt.

2. Cover the pot and bring the mixture to a boil over medium-high heat. Stir, reduce the heat to low, and simmer for 8 to 10 minutes, stirring occasionally, until the pasta is tender. Taste and adjust the seasonings as desired.

BLACK BEAN AND VEGGIE ENCHILADA ROTINI

SERVES 6

PREP TIME: 15 MINUTES | COOK TIME: 30 MINUTES

ALL-IN-ONE, VEGETARIAN

My son is a huge fan of enchiladas and requests them often. This pasta is a nod to that favorite, and it totally satisfies his craving. This saucy pasta is packed with veggies, hearty beans, and big flavors. But it's the toppings that really make it stand out. Avocado, a little cheese, and scallions make it go from "Wow" to *Amazing!*"

1 (28-ounce) can tomato purée

8 ounces dry rotini

1 (15.5-ounce) can black beans, rinsed and drained

1½ cups vegetable stock or broth

1 medium red, orange, or yellow bell pepper, diced

1 medium green bell pepper, diced

1 medium red onion, diced, plus more for serving (optional)

3 tablespoons chili powder

1 tablespoon ground cumin

1 teaspoon garlic powder

1 teaspoon salt

Shredded Cheddar cheese, for serving (optional)

Diced avocado, for serving (optional)

Crumbled tortilla chips, for serving (optional)

1. In a large pot or Dutch oven, combine the tomato purée, rotini, black beans, vegetable stock, bell peppers, onion, chili powder, cumin, garlic powder, and salt.

2. Cover the pot and bring the mixture to a boil over medium-high heat. Stir and reduce the heat to medium-low. Simmer for 16 to 20 minutes, stirring occasionally, until the pasta is tender.

3. Let the pasta sit for 5 minutes.

4. Taste and adjust the seasonings as desired. Serve topped with onions, Cheddar cheese, avocado, and tortilla chips (if using).

OPTION TIP: This is a great recipe to serve a crowd. Offer a toppings bar with 5 to 6 choices for guests. Consider adding crumbled queso fresco to the mix, too.

FRENCH ONION LINGUINE

SERVES 4

PREP TIME: 15 MINUTES | COOK TIME: 45 MINUTES

STEP-BY-STEP

French onion soup is a lovely dish that's full of flavor and nuance. And that nuance usually takes time to make—low and slow, as they say. But this pasta recipe, inspired by the ubiquitous soup, is also nuanced in flavor, except it's a little easier and a little more hands-off. If French onion soup is your thing, you'll want to try this pasta. It's rich and hearty and delightful with cheese melted on top.

2 tablespoons butter

2 pounds Vidalia onions, thinly sliced

½ teaspoon sugar

8 ounces dry linguine

1¾ cups beef stock

½ cup dry sherry

1 teaspoon dried thyme

1 teaspoon salt

Freshly grated Swiss or Gruyère cheese, for serving (optional)

OPTION TIP: Want to make this recipe over the top? Portion the prepared pasta into individual oven-safe dishes, sprinkle with the cheese, and broil for 1 to 2 minutes.

1. In a large pot or Dutch oven, melt the butter over medium heat. Add the onions and sprinkle with the sugar. Cook, stirring occasionally, for 15 to 20 minutes, until the onions are golden brown.

2. Add the linguine, beef stock, sherry, thyme, and salt to the pot. Cover the pot and bring the mixture to a boil over medium-high heat. Reduce the heat to low and simmer for 10 to 12 minutes, stirring occasionally, until the pasta is tender.

3. Top with Swiss cheese just before serving (if using).

RATATOUILLE ORZO

SERVES 4

PREP TIME: 15 MINUTES | COOK TIME: 25 MINUTES

ALL-IN-ONE, VEGAN

If summer could be summed up in one dish, this would be it. Eggplant, zucchini, tomatoes, bell peppers—it's all in here. If you happen to have it on hand, substitute 2 tablespoons finely chopped fresh basil for the dried basil for a real Mediterranean zing.

8 ounces dry orzo

1¼ cups vegetable stock

1 medium eggplant, peeled and cut into 1-inch pieces

1 medium sweet onion, roughly chopped

1 medium bell pepper (any color), cut into 1-inch pieces

1 medium zucchini, sliced into ¼-inch-thick slices

1 cup diced fresh tomatoes

3 garlic cloves, minced

2 teaspoons dried basil

1 teaspoon salt

½ teaspoon freshly ground black pepper

2 tablespoons balsamic vinegar

1. In a large pot or Dutch oven, combine the orzo, vegetable stock, eggplant, onion, bell pepper, zucchini, tomatoes, garlic, basil, salt, and black pepper. Stir.

2. Cover the pot and bring the mixture to a boil over medium-high heat. Reduce the heat to low and simmer for 10 to 12 minutes, stirring occasionally, until the pasta is tender.

3. Remove the pot from the heat. Stir in the balsamic vinegar.

4. Let the pasta sit for 5 minutes before serving.

INGREDIENT TIP: Use a good-quality balsamic vinegar—the label will usually say "D.O.C. Modena" on it. (Cheaper "balsamic" vinegar is made with ingredients like caramel color and sugar.) It will give the dish vibrancy and dimension without a lot of added acidity.

FRAGRANT SWEET POTATO AND RED ONION SHELLS

SERVES 4

PREP TIME: 10 MINUTES | COOK TIME: 35 MINUTES

STEP-BY-STEP, VEGAN

I was an adult when I first tried sweet potatoes. I fell in love with them and now enjoy them in many ways, like this pasta. With warm notes from cinnamon and sweet Hungarian paprika, as well as sweet potatoes, red onions, and napa cabbage, this pasta has an exotic feel to it—and a welcome one, at that.

2 tablespoons extra-virgin olive oil

1 (12-ounce) sweet potato, unpeeled and cut into ¾-inch pieces

1 medium red onion, diced

8 ounces dry medium shells

2 cups finely shredded and chopped napa cabbage

1¾ cups vegetable stock

½ cup apple juice

1 teaspoon dried rosemary

1 teaspoon salt

½ teaspoon ground cinnamon

½ teaspoon paprika

1. In a large pot or Dutch oven, heat the olive oil over medium heat. Add the sweet potato and onion and cook, stirring frequently, until the vegetables are softened and beginning to brown, about 8 to 10 minutes.

2. Add the shells, napa cabbage, vegetable stock, apple juice, rosemary, salt, cinnamon, and paprika to the pot.

3. Cover the pot and bring the mixture to a boil over medium heat. Reduce the heat to low and simmer for 10 to 12 minutes, stirring occasionally, until the pasta is tender.

4. Remove the pot from the heat. Let the pasta sit for 5 minutes before serving.

OPTION TIP: Mix in some diced grilled chicken for a full, all-in-one meal.

LEMON LOVERS' ZITI WITH GREEN BEANS

SERVES 4

PREP TIME: 10 MINUTES | COOK TIME: 20 MINUTES

ALL-IN-ONE, 30 MINUTES, VEGAN

Tart, bright lemon is mellowed (but only slightly) by the robust vegetable stock in this recipe. Use fresh green beans in this, as they will remain pleasantly al dente. This is a great dish to serve with grilled chicken.

8 ounces dry ziti
2 cups fresh green beans, cut into 1-inch pieces
1¾ cups vegetable stock
½ cup freshly squeezed lemon juice
2 garlic cloves, minced
1 teaspoon dried thyme
1 teaspoon salt
½ teaspoon freshly ground black pepper

SUBSTITUTION TIP: Wax beans can be substituted for the green beans for an equally flavorful dish. Or use a mixture of beans.

1. In a large pot or Dutch oven, combine the ziti, green beans, vegetable stock, lemon juice, garlic, thyme, salt, and black pepper.

2. Cover the pot and bring the mixture to a boil over medium-high heat. Reduce the heat to low and simmer for 10 to 12 minutes, stirring occasionally, until the pasta is tender.

3. Remove the pot from the heat. Uncover the pot and let the pasta sit for 5 minutes. Taste and adjust the seasonings as desired.

ASPARAGUS, SHALLOT, AND ROASTED RED PEPPER EGG NOODLES

SERVES 4

PREP TIME: 10 MINUTES | COOK TIME: 15 MINUTES

ALL-IN-ONE, 30 MINUTES, VEGETARIAN

Wide and delicate egg noodles are a lovely base for this pasta recipe featuring earthy, sweet, and sharp flavors. Thin stalks of asparagus are best for this veggie-filled noodle dish. You'll need about a half pound. For the red peppers, roast your own or buy jarred ones.

8 ounces dry wide egg noodles

2 cups water

1½ cups fresh 1-inch asparagus pieces

4 shallots, finely chopped

2 roasted red bell peppers, finely chopped

¼ cup vegetable stock

1 teaspoon salt

INGREDIENT TIP: Thin asparagus works best in this recipe. If using thicker asparagus, cut it into slimmer pieces.

1. In a large pot or Dutch oven, combine the egg noodles, water, asparagus, shallots, roasted red bell peppers, vegetable stock, and salt.

2. Cover the pot and bring the mixture to a boil over medium-high heat. Reduce the heat to low and simmer for 8 to 10 minutes, stirring occasionally, or until the pasta is tender.

3. Remove the pot from the heat. Stir. Let the pasta sit, uncovered, for 5 minutes before serving.

Chapter Four

MEAT PASTAS

Left: Sun-Dried Tomato, Chicken, and Garlic Pasta, page 50

PENNE WITH KIELBASA AND BEET GREENS

SERVES 4

PREP TIME: 10 MINUTES | COOK TIME: 25 MINUTES

ALL-IN-ONE

I love the flavor of kielbasa, and in this pasta recipe, it's just perfect. Earthy beet greens mingle with the salty kielbasa and sweet onions in this easy, tasty dish. Hearty and fresh, this is an excellent meal after a busy, stressful day.

8 ounces dry penne

4 cups coarsely chopped beet greens

1 precooked kielbasa sausage, cut into ¼-inch-thick slices

2 cups water

1 small yellow onion, quartered and thinly sliced

1 garlic clove, minced

SUBSTITUTION TIP: For a spicy take on this pasta, use chorizo sausage in place of the kielbasa. Cut it into chunks for best results.

1. In a large pot or Dutch oven, combine the penne, beet greens, kielbasa sausage, water, onion, and garlic. Stir.

2. Cover the pot and bring the mixture to a boil over high heat. Reduce the heat to low and simmer for 12 to 15 minutes, stirring occasionally, until the pasta is tender.

3. Remove the pot from the heat. Stir well. Taste and adjust the seasonings as desired.

LEMONY CHICKEN PASTA WITH BELL PEPPERS AND ONIONS

SERVES 4

PREP TIME: 15 MINUTES | COOK TIME: 30 MINUTES

STEP-BY-STEP

Each step in this pasta recipe helps build the complex and pleasant flavor of this pasta. This is perfect for fans of scampi, who'll recognize the flavors in this dish. It's excellent served with crusty bread and a tossed salad.

1 pound skinless, boneless chicken breast, cut into 1-inch pieces

1 tablespoon flour

½ teaspoon salt

½ teaspoon freshly ground black pepper

2 tablespoons extra-virgin olive oil

1 medium yellow onion, quartered and thinly sliced

1 medium red bell pepper, cut into strips and halved

1 medium green bell pepper, cut into strips and halved

2 garlic cloves, minced

8 ounces dry spaghetti

1½ cups chicken stock

1 lemon, juiced and zested

1. In a medium bowl, stir together the chicken, flour, salt, and black pepper.

2. In a large pot or Dutch oven, heat the olive oil over medium heat. Add the chicken and stir occasionally, until cooked through, about 5 to 7 minutes. Transfer the chicken to another medium bowl and set aside.

3. In the same pot, combine the onion, bell peppers, and garlic, and sauté for 5 to 7 minutes, until the vegetables are just beginning to get tender. Add the spaghetti, chicken stock, and lemon juice to the pot. Cover the pot and bring the mixture to a boil. Reduce the heat to low and simmer for 10 to 12 minutes, stirring occasionally, until the pasta is tender.

4. Stir in the chicken and lemon zest. Taste and adjust the seasonings as desired.

TIME-SAVING TIP: Raw chicken tenders can be substituted for the breast meat for a slight preparation time-saver. Cut them into 1-inch pieces.

DIRTY ORZO WITH ANDOUILLE SAUSAGE

SERVES 4

PREP TIME: 10 MINUTES | COOK TIME: 20 MINUTES

ALL-IN-ONE, 30 MINUTES

Fans of Creole cooking will enjoy the flavors of this pasta, which are similar to that of dirty rice. Spicy andouille sausage mingles with veggies and tiny orzo pasta in this creamy, flavorful dish. This is delightful served with Brown Sugar Cornbread (page 84).

8 ounces dry orzo

2¼ cups chicken broth

1 (6.25-ounce) cooked andouille sausage, diced

1 small red onion, diced

3 celery stalks, diced

1 medium green bell pepper, diced

1 medium tomato, diced

3 to 4 sprigs fresh thyme

INGREDIENT TIP: The key to this recipe is all the ingredients being similar in size so the flavors and textures mingle well. Try to dice all the veggies roughly the same size.

1. In a large pot or Dutch oven, combine the orzo, chicken broth, sausage, onion, celery, bell pepper, tomato, and thyme. Stir.

2. Cover the pot and bring the mixture to a boil over medium-high heat. Stir, reduce the heat to low, and simmer for 12 to 15 minutes, stirring occasionally, until the orzo is tender.

3. Remove the pot from the heat. Taste and adjust the seasonings as desired.

SPAGHETTI WITH MEAT SAUCE

SERVES 4

PREP TIME: 10 MINUTES | COOK TIME: 30 MINUTES

STEP-BY-STEP

As far as good dishes for cold days go, this one is excellent. Hearty meat sauce makes this bone-warming pasta a family favorite. Serve it with crusty bread—or, better yet, Garlic Bread (page 85).

1 tablespoon extra-virgin olive oil
1 pound ground beef
1 small onion, diced
1 small green bell pepper, diced
1 (28-ounce) can crushed tomatoes
8 ounces dry thin spaghetti
1½ cups water
2 garlic cloves, minced
1 teaspoon dried basil
1 teaspoon dried oregano
1 teaspoon salt
1 dried bay leaf

1. In a large pot or Dutch oven, heat the olive oil over medium heat. Add the ground beef, onion, and green bell pepper and sauté until the ground beef is browned, 5 to 7 minutes. Drain any excess fat.

2. Add the crushed tomatoes, spaghetti (break it in half to fit, if needed), water, garlic, basil, oregano, salt, and bay leaf.

3. Cover the pot and bring the mixture to a boil. Reduce the heat to low and cook, covered, for 8 to 10 minutes, stirring every 2 to 3 minutes, until the pasta is tender and most of the liquid has evaporated.

4. Uncover the pot and cook for an additional 2 to 3 minutes, until the sauce reaches your desired thickness.

5. Stir well. Taste and adjust the seasonings as desired.

INGREDIENT TIP: With recipes that have multiple steps, like this one, I like to measure everything before I begin. For the seasonings, I combine them in a small glass bowl so I can dump them all into the pot at once when the time comes, instead of fumbling with containers and measuring spoons.

CHICKEN PARMESAN

SERVES 4

PREP TIME: 15 MINUTES | COOK TIME: 35 MINUTES

STEP-BY-STEP

Chicken Parmesan lovers will enjoy this noodle-based take on the Italian-American classic. Cubed and breaded chicken is fried until it is tender and golden. Then pasta is cooked in its sauce. Stir the cooked chicken in, top with cheese, and voilà! This is appropriately cheesy and saucy, but way easier to make than the traditional version.

1 pound skinless, boneless chicken breast, cut into 1-inch pieces
2 tablespoons dried bread crumbs
1 teaspoon cornstarch
2 tablespoons extra-virgin olive oil
1 (28-ounce) can crushed tomatoes
1 (15.5-ounce) can diced tomatoes, undrained
8 ounces dry ziti
1 cup water
3 garlic cloves, minced
1 teaspoon dried basil
1 teaspoon dried oregano
1 teaspoon salt
1 dried bay leaf
1 cup shredded mozzarella cheese

1. In a medium bowl, stir together the chicken, bread crumbs, and cornstarch.

2. In a large pot or Dutch oven, heat the olive oil over medium heat. Add the chicken, discarding any excess bread crumbs. Cook, stirring often, until the chicken is browned and cooked through, about 8 to 10 minutes. Transfer the chicken to another medium bowl and set aside.

3. In the same pot, combine the crushed tomatoes, diced tomatoes, ziti, water, garlic, basil, oregano, salt, and bay leaf.

4. Cover the pot and bring the mixture to a boil. Reduce the heat to low and cook, covered, for 12 to 14 minutes, stirring every 2 to 3 minutes, until the pasta is tender and most of the liquid has evaporated.

5. Stir in the chicken. Sprinkle with the mozzarella cheese. Re-cover the pot and cook for an additional 3 to 5 minutes, until the cheese is fully melted.

OPTION TIP: For a fancier take on this pasta, after stirring in the chicken, divide the mixture between 4 oven-safe dishes. Top each with ¼ cup shredded mozzarella cheese. Broil for 2 to 3 minutes, until the cheese is melted. Serve immediately.

SAUSAGE AND BELL PEPPER PASTA

SERVES 4

PREP TIME: 10 MINUTES | COOK TIME: 20 MINUTES

ALL-IN-ONE, 30 MINUTES

The combination of Italian sausages, bell peppers, and marinara sauce reminds me of my childhood. My grandmother would sometimes make large trays of sausage and bell peppers when our whole family was coming for dinner. This dish is an ode to that memory, and is a favorite of my kids.

1 (28-ounce) can crushed tomatoes

1 (12-ounce) package precooked Italian chicken sausage, cut into ¼-inch-thick slices

8 ounces dry fettuccine

1½ cups water

1 large green bell pepper, thinly sliced

1 medium yellow onion, halved and thinly sliced

2 garlic cloves, minced

1 teaspoon dried basil

1 teaspoon dried oregano

1 teaspoon salt

1 dried bay leaf

1. In a large pot or Dutch oven, combine the crushed tomatoes, Italian sausage, fettuccine, water, bell pepper, onion, garlic, basil, oregano, salt, and bay leaf.

2. Cover the pot and bring the mixture to a boil over high heat. Reduce the heat to low and simmer for 10 to 12 minutes, stirring occasionally, until the pasta is tender.

3. Taste and adjust the seasonings as desired.

SUBSTITUTION TIP: If you prefer the more traditional sweet or hot Italian sausage, you can substitute either for the chicken sausage. However, it should be cooked first.

HAM AND PEA FARFALLE

SERVES 4

PREP TIME: 5 MINUTES | COOK TIME: 25 MINUTES

ALL-IN-ONE, 30 MINUTES, QUICK PREP

My grandfather introduced me to split pea soup one fall day when he brought soups for everyone at our house. The flavors were a revelation—sweet, smoky, salty, and earthy all at once. This pasta is inspired by that memory of split pea soup.

8 ounces dry farfalle

7 ounces ham steak, cubed

1¼ cups chicken stock

1 cup fresh or frozen peas

1 cup water

⅔ cup grated carrots

2 shallots, quartered and thinly sliced

1 garlic clove, minced

1 teaspoon salt

INGREDIENT TIP: Got fresh peas? For best results, cook them first before using them in this recipe. This is best made with a smoked ham steak.

1. In a large pot or Dutch oven, combine the farfalle, ham, chicken stock, peas, water, carrots, shallots, garlic, and salt.

2. Cover the pot and bring the mixture to a boil over high heat. Reduce the heat to low and simmer for 12 to 14 minutes, until the pasta is tender, stirring occasionally.

3. Let the pasta sit for 5 minutes before serving.

SLOPPY JOE PENNE

SERVES 4

PREP TIME: 5 MINUTES | COOK TIME: 30 MINUTES

STEP-BY-STEP, QUICK PREP

Food should be fun and nourishing. This is both. That favorite sandwich—the messy, drippy sloppy joe—gets a fun makeover in this pasta recipe. It has all the flavor of the deli classic, but without the mess.

1 tablespoon extra-virgin olive oil
1 medium Vidalia onion, diced
1 pound ground beef
2 cups water
1 (6-ounce) can tomato purée
2 tablespoons balsamic vinegar
3 tablespoons light brown sugar
2 tablespoons molasses
1 teaspoon smoked paprika
1 teaspoon garlic powder
1 teaspoon salt
8 ounces dry penne

1. In a large pot or Dutch oven, heat the olive oil over medium heat. Add the onion and cook, stirring occasionally, until it to brown, about 8 to 10 minutes. Add the ground beef and brown thoroughly, 5 to 7 minutes. Drain any excess fat.

2. Add the water, tomato purée, balsamic vinegar, brown sugar, molasses, smoked paprika, garlic powder, and salt to the pot. Stir. Add the penne.

3. Cover the pot and bring the mixture to a boil. Reduce the heat to low and simmer for 10 to 12 minutes, stirring occasionally, until the pasta is tender.

4. Remove the pot from the heat. Taste and adjust the seasonings as desired.

SUBSTITUTION TIP: Ground beef is used in this recipe but it can easily be traded for ground turkey or ground pork. Ground chicken, which tends to be softer, could work too, though the consistency of the sauce will be altered.

LOADED TACO ROTINI

SERVES 4

PREP TIME: 5 MINUTES | COOK TIME: 25 MINUTES

STEP-BY-STEP, 30 MINUTES, QUICK PREP

Taco Tuesday is a thing in my house, but I am always looking for creative ways to enjoy tacos without serving the same tacos week after week. This pasta is a great alternative. My taco-loving family cannot get enough of this when I make it. I love serving it with a variety of toppings so everyone can customize their own bowl.

1 pound ground beef
8 ounces dry rotini
2 cups water
1 (15.5-ounce) can diced tomatoes, undrained
2 tablespoons chili powder
2 teaspoons garlic powder
2 teaspoons ground cumin
1 teaspoon salt
Roughly chopped avocado, for serving
Salsa, for serving
Shredded Cheddar cheese, for serving
Shredded lettuce, for serving

1. Heat a large pot or Dutch oven over medium heat. Add the ground beef and cook, breaking it apart, until browned, 5 to 7 minutes. Drain any excess fat.

2. Add the rotini, water, tomatoes, chili powder, garlic powder, cumin, and salt. Cover the pot and bring the mixture to a boil over high heat. Reduce the heat to low and simmer for 10 to 12 minutes, stirring occasionally, until the pasta is tender.

3. Remove the pot from the heat. Serve the pasta topped with the avocado, salsa, Cheddar cheese, and lettuce.

OPTION TIP: Although I make several suggestions for toppings, don't limit yourself. Diced red onions, sour cream, crumbled queso fresco, guacamole, tortilla chips, diced fresh tomatoes—there are so many options for topping this.

CILANTRO-LIME STEAK FAJITA PASTA

SERVES 4

PREP TIME: 10 MINUTES | COOK TIME: 35 MINUTES

STEP-BY-STEP

By cooking this pasta dish in stages, a combination of flavors and textures can create something amazing. Perfectly cooked steak makes this meal. And the combination of cilantro and lime gives this dish a fresh tartness that brings everything together.

1½ pounds sirloin steak tips
Salt
Freshly ground black pepper
8 ounces dry linguine
2 cups water
1 medium green bell pepper, thinly sliced
1 medium red bell pepper, thinly sliced
1 medium Vidalia onion, halved and thinly sliced
1 lime, juiced and zested
½ teaspoon ground cumin
1 tablespoon finely chopped fresh cilantro

1. Heat a large pot or Dutch oven over medium heat. Season the steak tips all over with salt and black pepper. Add the steak tips to the pot and cook, turning, until they are browned on all sides to the desired doneness, about 10 to 15 minutes. Transfer the steak tips to a medium bowl and set aside.

2. In the same pot, combine the linguine, water, bell peppers, onion, lime juice and zest, and cumin.

3. Cover the pot and bring the mixture to a boil over high heat. Reduce the heat to low and simmer for 10 to 12 minutes, stirring occasionally, until the pasta is tender.

4. Remove the pot from the heat. Stir in the cilantro. Slice the steak tips into thin slices. Stir them into the pasta.

SUBSTITUTION TIP: If you can't find steak tips, which are long strips of steak, don't despair. You can substitute sirloin steak. Simply cut it into 1-inch-thick strips before cooking.

SUN-DRIED TOMATO, CHICKEN, AND GARLIC PASTA

SERVES 4
PREP TIME: 15 MINUTES | COOK TIME: 30 MINUTES
STEP-BY-STEP

Winner, winner, sun-dried tomato and chicken dinner! This hearty pasta has big, bold flavors—pungent garlic, sweet sun-dried tomatoes, and herbaceous basil. Combined with sautéed chicken and a delicate white wine pasta sauce, it's a delightful dinner.

1 tablespoon unsalted butter
1 pound chicken tenders, cut into
    1-inch pieces
1 tablespoon flour
Salt
Freshly ground black pepper
8 ounces dry farfalle
2 cups water
¼ cup white wine
3 ounces thinly sliced sun-dried tomatoes
4 garlic cloves, minced
2 tablespoons thinly sliced fresh basil

1. In a large pot or Dutch oven, melt the butter over medium heat. Meanwhile, in a medium bowl, stir together the chicken, flour, and a little salt and black pepper. Add the chicken to the pot and cook through, stirring occasionally, about 8 to 10 minutes. Transfer the chicken to another medium bowl and set aside.

2. In the same pot, combine the farfalle, water, white wine, sun-dried tomatoes, and garlic.

3. Cover the pot and bring the mixture to a boil over high heat. Reduce the heat to low and simmer for 12 to 14 minutes, stirring occasionally, until the pasta is tender.

4. Remove the pot from the heat. Stir in the chicken and basil. Taste and adjust the seasonings as desired.

SUBSTITUTION TIP: Can't find raw chicken tenders? Substitute chicken breast. Cut it into 1-inch cubes before using.

CHEESEBURGER MACARONI

SERVES 4

PREP TIME: 5 MINUTES | COOK TIME: 35 MINUTES

STEP-BY-STEP, QUICK PREP

A certain boxed pasta "helper" was a family dinner staple when I was in middle school. While I won't turn to that box these days, I love making homemade versions like this cheeseburger macaroni. With a creamy, cheesy sauce, bold burger flavor, and small pasta shapes, this pasta is fun to eat.

1 pound ground beef

1 teaspoon smoked paprika

1 teaspoon garlic powder

1 teaspoon kosher salt

8 ounces dry elbow macaroni or small shells

1¼ cups water

1 cup shredded sharp Cheddar cheese

1 cup milk

1 tablespoon unsalted butter

1 teaspoon ground mustard

1. In a large pot or Dutch oven, brown the ground beef over medium heat for 5 to 7 minutes. Drain any excess fat. Season with the paprika, garlic powder, and salt. Stir well. Add the macaroni, water, Cheddar, milk, butter, and ground mustard to the pot. Stir to combine.

2. Cover the pot and bring the mixture to a boil over high heat. Reduce the heat to low and simmer for 10 to 12 minutes, stirring every few minutes, until the pasta is tender.

3. Remove the pot from the heat and let the pasta sit for 5 minutes. Taste and adjust the seasonings as needed.

OPTION TIP: For an even creamier version of this pasta, stir in 2 tablespoons heavy cream after removing the pot from the heat. It's decadent!

STEAK RIGATONI WITH ARUGULA

SERVES 4

PREP TIME: 5 MINUTES | COOK TIME: 35 MINUTES

STEP-BY-STEP, QUICK PREP

This recipe calls for a cut of thinly sliced beef called shaved steak. It is most often used for cheesesteak sandwiches, but also excellent in dishes like this. The thin, small pieces brown nicely and incorporate into the pasta so well. This pasta has a rich flavor that's lovely on a cold night.

1 pound shaved steak
Salt
Freshly ground black pepper
½ teaspoon garlic powder
½ teaspoon paprika
8 ounces dry rigatoni
1 small sweet onion, diced
1¼ cups water
1 cup beef broth
2 cups fresh arugula

1. Heat a large pot or Dutch oven over medium heat. Add the shaved steak and season with the salt, black pepper, garlic powder, and paprika. Cook, stirring and breaking the steak apart, until browned, 5 to 7 minutes. Add the rigatoni, onion, water, and beef broth. Stir to combine.

2. Cover the pot and bring the mixture to a boil over high heat. Reduce the heat to low and simmer for 10 to 12 minutes, stirring occasionally, until the pasta is tender.

3. Remove the pot from the heat and stir in the arugula. Taste and adjust the seasonings as needed.

OPTION TIP: For an even more robust flavor, substitute ¼ cup of the water with red wine.

Chapter Five

SEAFOOD PASTAS

Left: Lemon-Garlic Shrimp Pasta with Arugula, page 59

FETTUCCINE WITH MUSSELS AND TOMATOES

SERVES 4

PREP TIME: 5 MINUTES | COOK TIME: 20 MINUTES

ALL-IN-ONE, 30 MINUTES, QUICK PREP

Whenever I have guests over, I like to serve dishes that look impressive but are really simple to make. It means less stress for me and more fun for everyone. This pasta, perfect for small gatherings, is ridiculously easy to make. But your guests don't need to know that!

8 ounces dry fettuccine

2 cups halved grape tomatoes

2 cups water

2 shallots, quartered and sliced into ¼-inch-thick pieces

5 garlic cloves, minced

¼ cup white wine

1 tablespoon unsalted butter

1 teaspoon salt

⅛ teaspoon freshly ground black pepper

2 pounds mussels, cleaned thoroughly

1. In a large pot or Dutch oven, combine the fettuccine, tomatoes, water, shallots, garlic, white wine, butter, salt, and black pepper.

2. Cover the pot and bring the mixture to a boil over high heat. Add the mussels and re-cover the pot. Reduce the heat to low and cook, stirring occasionally, until the pasta is tender and the mussels are open, about 10 to 12 minutes. Discard any unopened mussels.

3. Taste and adjust the seasonings as desired.

INGREDIENT TIP: Mussels sometimes have a stringy bit called a beard. Use a knife to scrape this away before cooking.

PAPPARDELLE WITH RED CLAM SAUCE

SERVES 4

PREP TIME: 5 MINUTES | COOK TIME: 20 MINUTES

ALL-IN-ONE, 30 MINUTES, QUICK PREP

I've spent much of my life near the coast, where seafood is fresh and abundant. I've been clamming, eaten oysters harvested mere hours before, and consumed more varieties of fish than a supermarket aisle would have you believe existed. And I love clams in all forms, including red clam sauce. This version uses canned clams instead of fresh, but you could substitute 2 pounds of littleneck clams instead. This saucy pasta is super easy to make.

8 ounces dry pappardelle

2 cups water

1 (15.5-ounce) can diced tomatoes, undrained

1 (6-ounce) can tomato paste

2 shallots, quartered and sliced

3 garlic cloves, sliced

2 (6.5-ounce) cans minced clams, undrained

1 dried bay leaf

1 teaspoon dried basil

1 teaspoon dried thyme

1 teaspoon salt

1. In a large pot or Dutch oven, combine the pappardelle, water, tomatoes, tomato paste, shallots, garlic, clams, bay leaf, basil, thyme, and salt.

2. Cover the pot and bring the mixture to a boil over high heat. Reduce the heat to low and cook, stirring occasionally, for 8 to 10 minutes, until the pasta is tender.

3. Remove the pot from the heat and uncover. Let the pasta sit for 5 minutes before serving.

SUBSTITUTION TIP: Fresh herbs are great in this pasta, too. Substitute 1 tablespoon fresh minced basil and 1 tablespoon fresh minced thyme for the dried herbs, if desired.

LOBSTER LINGUINE WITH ARUGULA

SERVES 4

PREP TIME: 5 MINUTES | COOK TIME: 25 MINUTES

ALL-IN-ONE, 30 MINUTES, QUICK PREP

Buttery, satisfying and decadent, this pasta is a delight. Fresh lobster is best (and can be least expensive when you're willing to shell it yourself), but frozen lobster can be used as well. If you've ever had lobster Newburg, you might just recognize the flavors. Serve this with biscuits for sopping up the sauce.

8 ounces dry linguine
1¼ cups water
½ cup sherry
½ cup milk
2 tablespoons butter
1 garlic clove, minced
1 teaspoon salt
½ teaspoon paprika
¼ teaspoon freshly ground black pepper
¾ cup (4 ounces) roughly chopped lobster meat from 1 (1¼-pound) lobster
1 cup roughly chopped fresh arugula
2 tablespoons heavy cream (optional)

1. In a large pot or Dutch oven, combine the linguine, water, sherry, milk, butter, garlic, salt, paprika, and black pepper. Stir well.

2. Cover the pot and bring the mixture to a boil over high heat. Reduce the heat to low and simmer for 12 to 14 minutes, stirring occasionally, until the pasta is tender.

3. Remove the pot from the heat. Stir in the lobster, arugula, and heavy cream (if using). Cover the pot and let the pasta sit for 5 minutes. Taste and adjust the seasonings as desired.

SAFETY TIP: It is absolutely critical that you stir the ingredients together before you begin cooking. Sherry is extremely flammable and will ignite if not combined with the other ingredients. A simple stir takes care of everything.

LEMON-GARLIC SHRIMP PASTA WITH ARUGULA

SERVES 4
PREP TIME: 15 MINUTES | COOK TIME: 30 MINUTES
STEP-BY-STEP

By cooking the shrimp first while making this recipe, they are rendered perfectly cooked, not tough and chewy. Then the egg noodles are cooked with the bright notes of lemon, garlic, and peppery arugula, giving this pasta great flavor. Serve with grated Parmesan for sprinkling.

1 tablespoon extra-virgin olive oil
1 pound raw shrimp, peeled and deveined
1 teaspoon salt, plus more for seasoning
Freshly ground black pepper
3 garlic cloves, minced
8 ounces dry wide egg noodles
2 cups water
1 lemon, zested and juiced
1 cup arugula

1. In a large pot or Dutch oven, heat the olive oil over medium heat. Add the shrimp and season with salt and black pepper. Cook, stirring, until the shrimp are pink all over, about 5 to 7 minutes. Transfer the shrimp to a medium bowl and set aside.

2. In the same pot, cook the garlic until fragrant, about 1 minute. Stir in the egg noodles, water, and lemon zest and juice, along with 1 teaspoon salt.

3. Cover the pot and bring the mixture to a boil over high heat. Reduce the heat to low and simmer for 10 to 12 minutes, stirring occasionally, until the pasta is tender.

4. Remove the pot from the heat and stir in the shrimp and arugula. Cover the pot and let the pasta sit for 5 minutes before serving.

INGREDIENT TIP: The bigger the shrimp, the better. Though you could certainly make this with any size shrimp, jumbo shrimp work best.

SMOKED SALMON AND DILL ROTINI WITH ONIONS AND CAPERS

My son likens this pasta to a bagel and lox, just without the bagel and the cream cheese. My daughter just says it's really good. Fans of smoked salmon will enjoy the flavors here. Salty capers, fresh dill, and smoky salmon are a lovely combination.

1 tablespoon extra-virgin olive oil

1 small sweet onion, diced

½ teaspoon salt, plus more for seasoning

Freshly ground black pepper

8 ounces dry rotini

1¾ cups water

½ cup white wine

4 ounces smoked salmon, roughly chopped

2 tablespoons finely chopped fresh dill

2 tablespoons capers

OPTION TIP: This pasta can be made ahead and served later. To do so, prepare the pasta, but don't add the smoked salmon or dill. Store the mixture in an airtight container, reheat it completely, and stir in the smoked salmon and dill just before serving.

1. In a large pot or Dutch oven, heat the olive oil over medium heat. Add the onion and season with salt and black pepper. Cook, stirring occasionally, for 8 to 10 minutes, until the onion is golden brown.

2. Add the rotini, water, and white wine to the pot, along with ½ teaspoon salt. Cover the pot and bring the mixture to a boil over high heat. Reduce the heat to low and cook for 10 to 12 minutes, stirring occasionally, until the pasta is tender.

3. Remove the pot from the heat. Stir in the salmon, dill, and capers.

TERIYAKI SHRIMP SOBA NOODLES

SERVES 4

PREP TIME: 10 MINUTES | COOK TIME: 25 MINUTES

STEP-BY-STEP

Bold and packed with veggies, this pasta is a delicious ode to big flavors and really highlights the shrimp. The rich sauce brings together all the textures and flavors. Got leftovers? This reheats well.

1 tablespoon extra-virgin olive oil
1 pound shrimp, peeled and deveined
Salt
Freshly ground black pepper
8 ounces dry soba noodles
1 cup water (plus more as needed)
1 cup fresh green beans, cut into
    1-inch pieces
1 cup shredded napa cabbage
½ to ¾ cup diced carrots
½ cup soy sauce
1 tablespoon peeled and grated
    fresh ginger
1 garlic clove, minced
1 tablespoon brown sugar

1. In a large pot or Dutch oven, heat the olive oil over medium heat. Add the shrimp and season with salt and black pepper. Sauté for 5 to 8 minutes, until the shrimp are opaque. Transfer them to a medium bowl and set aside.

2. In the same pot, combine the soba noodles, water, green beans, napa cabbage, carrots, soy sauce, ginger, garlic, and brown sugar.

3. Cover the pot and bring the mixture to a boil over high heat. Reduce the heat to low and simmer for 8 to 10 minutes, stirring occasionally, until the noodles are tender. If the sauce seems too thick halfway through the cooking time, add ¼ cup water. The sauce needs to be loose for the pasta to properly cook.

4. Remove the pot from the heat. Stir in the reserved shrimp.

OPTION TIP: For extra teriyaki flavor, finish off each serving of this pasta with a drizzle of teriyaki glaze. It's a lovely addition.

THREE-CHEESE LOBSTER
MAC AND CHEESE

SERVES 4
PREP TIME: 10 MINUTES | COOK TIME: 20 MINUTES
ALL-IN-ONE, 30 MINUTES

On a trip to Boston one winter, my family happened into a seafood restaurant, where my son and I ordered the creamiest lobster mac and cheese I'd ever had. This recipe was created with that dish in mind. Filled with bold flavors, this creamy mac-aroni and cheese is a treat. It's best served as soon as it's done cooking.

8 ounces dry elbow macaroni
1 cup water
1 cup milk
⅓ cup freshly grated aged Gouda cheese
⅓ cup freshly grated Parmesan cheese
⅓ cup shredded Cheddar cheese
¼ cup sherry
1 teaspoon salt
1 teaspoon ground mustard
¾ to 1 cup (about 4 ounces)
   chopped lobster meat from
   1 (1¼-pound) lobster
2 tablespoons heavy cream

1. In a large pot or Dutch oven, combine the macaroni, water, milk, Gouda, Parme-san, Cheddar, sherry, salt, and mustard. Stir well.

2. Cover the pot and bring the mixture to a boil over high heat. Reduce the heat to low and simmer for 10 to 12 minutes, stirring occasionally, until the pasta is tender.

3. Remove the pot from the heat and stir in the lobster and heavy cream. Let the pasta sit for 5 minutes before serving.

INGREDIENT TIP: Stirring when the ingredients are added to the pot is extremely important. You need to mix the sherry into the other ingredients; other-wise, it may flame when you remove the lid to stir once the mixture is cooking.

FETTUCCINE WITH WHITE CLAM SAUCE

SERVES 4

PREP TIME: 5 MINUTES | COOK TIME: 20 MINUTES

ALL-IN-ONE, 30 MINUTES, QUICK PREP

Heavy pastas are wonderful for chilly days because they bring a lot of warmth in their bulk. But for other days, fresh and light pastas like this one are a delight. This vibrant pasta is rich with the flavor of clams, and a hint of lemon. Serve it with toasty bread.

8 ounces dry fettuccine

2 (6.5-ounce) cans minced or chopped clams in clam juice, undrained

1 cup water

1 cup chicken stock

2 garlic cloves, minced

1 teaspoon salt

⅛ teaspoon red pepper flakes

1 to 2 tablespoons freshly squeezed lemon juice

2 tablespoons finely chopped fresh parsley

Lemon wedges, for garnish

INGREDIENT TIP: In my opinion, the red pepper flakes make this dish. But if you aren't a fan of spicy food, omit them.

1. In a large pot or Dutch oven, combine the fettuccine, clams, water, chicken stock, garlic, salt, and red pepper flakes.

2. Cover the pot and bring the mixture to a boil over high heat. Reduce the heat to low and simmer for 12 to 14 minutes, until the pasta is tender. Remove the pot from the heat and stir in the lemon juice. Sprinkle with the parsley. Serve with lemon wedges.

GORGONZOLA AND SHRIMP RIGATONI WITH PEAS

SERVES 4
PREP TIME: 10 MINUTES | COOK TIME: 20 MINUTES
ALL-IN-ONE, 30 MINUTES

On the day my son started kindergarten, I rose early to make him his favorite Gorgonzola shrimp pasta to take for lunch. Yes, he was the kid with seafood at the lunch table, and he was proud of it. This recipe is an easier take on that old favorite.

1 pound shrimp, peeled and deveined
8 ounces dry rigatoni
1½ cups water
1 cup frozen peas
1 cup milk
1 teaspoon salt
1 teaspoon dried thyme
½ teaspoon garlic powder
½ cup crumbled Gorgonzola cheese
¼ cup thinly sliced fresh basil

OPTION TIP: Fresh peas can be substituted in this recipe but need to be cooked first. Boil them until tender and then add as directed to this recipe.

1. In a large pot or Dutch oven, combine the shrimp, rigatoni, water, peas, milk, salt, thyme, and garlic powder.

2. Cover the pot and bring the mixture to a boil over high heat. Reduce the heat to low and simmer for 12 to 14 minutes, stirring occasionally, until the shrimp are opaque and the pasta is tender. Remove the pot from the heat and stir in the Gorgonzola cheese and basil.

DECONSTRUCTED CRAB CAKE MACARONI

SERVES 4

PREP TIME: 5 MINUTES: | COOK TIME: 15 MINUTES

ALL-IN-ONE, 30 MINUTES, QUICK PREP

The first time I had crab cakes was while on vacation in southern New Jersey with my friend's family. The slightly sweet crab meat with spices and bread crumbs won me over. I have taken those flavors and packed them into this pasta dish. Fans of crab cakes will want to try it.

8 ounces dry elbow macaroni

2 (6-ounce) cans crab meat, drained

1 cup chicken stock

1 cup water

4 scallions, white and green parts, thinly sliced

2 tablespoons freshly squeezed lemon juice

1 teaspoon Worcestershire sauce

1 teaspoon ground mustard

½ teaspoon garlic powder

1 teaspoon salt

2 tablespoons dried bread crumbs

1. In a large pot or Dutch oven, combine the macaroni, crab meat, chicken stock, water, scallions, lemon juice, Worcestershire sauce, mustard, garlic powder, and salt.

2. Cover the pot and bring the mixture to a boil over high heat. Reduce the heat to low and simmer for 8 to 10 minutes, stirring occasionally, until the pasta is tender.

3. Remove the pot from the heat and stir in the bread crumbs.

OPTION TIP: For a fancier presentation, serve this with lemon wedges and thinly sliced scallions (or the dark green parts of the scallions) sprinkled on top.

SEARED TUNA AND AVOCADO FARFALLE WITH SCALLION SOY SAUCE

SERVES 4

PREP TIME: 10 MINUTES | COOK TIME: 30 MINUTES

STEP-BY-STEP

What if your favorite sushi roll could become a pasta? It can with this recipe. Seared tuna is combined with snow peas, scallions, and a lovely soy-based sauce. Fresh avocado finishes it off with an element of creaminess. This is best eaten immediately after making it.

8 ounces fresh tuna steaks

Salt

Freshly ground black pepper

8 ounces dry farfalle

2 cups water

1 cup snow peas, cut into 1-inch pieces

3 scallions, white and light green parts thinly sliced and separated from the dark green parts, divided

¼ cup rice vinegar

1 tablespoon peeled and grated fresh ginger

1 teaspoon fish sauce

2 tablespoons soy sauce

1 teaspoon honey

1 avocado, cut into chunks

1. Heat a large pot or Dutch oven over medium-high heat. Season the tuna steaks all over with salt and black pepper. Sear the tuna in the pot for 2 to 3 minutes per side, to your desired doneness. Transfer the tuna to a plate and set aside.

2. In the same pot, combine the farfalle, water, snow peas, white and light green parts of the scallions, rice vinegar, ginger, and fish sauce.

3. Cover the pot and bring the mixture to a boil over high heat. Reduce the heat to low and simmer for 10 to 12 minutes, stirring occasionally, until the pasta is tender.

4. Remove the pot from the heat and stir in the soy sauce, honey, tuna, and avocado. Taste and adjust the seasonings as desired. Sprinkle with the dark green parts of the scallions.

INGREDIENT TIP: Wait to stir in the avocado and tuna until you are ready to serve this for best results.

KOREAN BARBECUE-INSPIRED SHRIMP PASTA

SERVES 4
PREP TIME: 10 MINUTES | COOK TIME: 20 MINUTES
STEP-BY-STEP, 30 MINUTES

For those who like dishes with bite, this pasta is bold and impressive, with a bit of spiciness, too. The shrimp are cooked first, allowing them to be perfectly prepared—overcooked shrimp are the bane of cooking!

1 tablespoon extra-virgin olive oil

1 pound large shrimp, peeled and deveined

1 tablespoon sriracha sauce

1 tablespoon honey

1 tablespoon mirin or seasoned rice vinegar

1 tablespoon soy sauce

½ teaspoon toasted sesame oil

2 garlic cloves, minced, divided

1 teaspoon peeled and grated fresh ginger, divided

8 ounces dry angel hair

1¼ cups water

1 cup julienned carrots

1 cup roughly chopped kale

1 cup vegetable stock

1 teaspoon salt

1. In a large nonstick pot or Dutch oven, heat the olive oil over medium heat. Add the shrimp and cook for 2 to 3 minutes, until they to turn pink.

2. Add the sriracha sauce, honey, mirin, soy sauce, sesame oil, 1 of the garlic cloves, and ½ teaspoon of the ginger. Stir well. Continue cooking until the shrimp are cooked through, 2 to 3 minutes. Transfer the shrimp and as much of the sauce as you can to a medium bowl and set aside.

3. In the same pot, combine the angel hair, water, carrots, kale, vegetable stock, and salt. Cover the pot and bring the mixture to a boil over high heat. Reduce the heat to low and simmer for 6 to 8 minutes, stirring occasionally, until the pasta is tender.

4. Remove the pot from the heat. Divide the pasta evenly among 4 bowls or plates. Top each serving with one-fourth of the shrimp and sauce.

INGREDIENT TIP: Angel hair pasta cooks very quickly. Be sure not to overcook it.

SPICY CRAB PARMESAN ZITI

SERVES 4

PREP TIME: 10 MINUTES | COOK TIME: 20 MINUTES

STEP-BY-STEP, 30 MINUTES

Sweet crab, spicy jalapeño, bright garlic, and verdant parsley with a finish of Parmesan cheese. This pasta dish is perfect for those who like dishes with bite.

2 tablespoons extra-virgin olive oil
4 garlic cloves, minced
1 jalapeño, minced
8 ounces dry ziti
2¼ cups water
1 (6-ounce) can crab meat, undrained
1 teaspoon salt
⅓ cup finely chopped fresh parsley
1 cup freshly grated Parmesan cheese

OPTION TIP: This freezes and reheats well. Divide it into portion-size bags and freeze. When ready to eat, defrost a portion overnight in the fridge and then transfer it to a microwave-safe bowl. Heat for 1 to 2 minutes on high, stirring once, until cooked through.

1. In a large pot or Dutch oven, heat the olive oil over medium heat. Add the garlic and jalapeño and cook for 1 to 2 minutes, until the mixture is fragrant. Do not let it brown.

2. Add the ziti, water, crab, and salt to the pot. Cover the pot and bring the mixture to a boil over high heat. Reduce the heat to low and simmer for 10 to 12 minutes, stirring occasionally, until the pasta is tender.

3. Remove the pot from the heat and stir in the parsley and Parmesan cheese.

Chapter Six

SALADS AND SIDES

Left: Roasted Beets with Feta and Onions, page 80, and Panzanella Salad, page 76

ARUGULA SALAD WITH STRAWBERRIES AND PEPITAS

SERVES 4

PREP TIME: 10 MINUTES

VEGAN

Salad doesn't have to mean a bag of lettuce mixed with tomatoes and cucumbers, though that can be tasty. Step outside the salad box by using a variety of greens and changing up the mix-ins! Peppery arugula, sweet strawberries, and salty pepitas meet in this easy, flavorful salad.

4 cups arugula
1 cup quartered fresh strawberries
¼ cup pepitas (roasted, salted, hulled pumpkin seeds)
2 tablespoons balsamic vinegar
1 tablespoon extra-virgin olive oil
Salt
Freshly ground black pepper

In a medium serving bowl, toss together the arugula, strawberries, pepitas, balsamic vinegar, and olive oil. Season with salt and black pepper. Serve immediately.

SUBSTITUTION TIP: Can't find pepitas? Try using chopped walnuts or pecans instead.

TOMATO, APPLE, AND RED ONION SALAD

SERVES 4

PREP TIME: 10 MINUTES

VEGAN

This recipe is best made in late summer and early fall when the tomatoes, basil, and apples are at their freshest. But on harsh winter days, this salad can be a lovely reminder of summertime as well. Be sure to choose a crisp, sweet apple.

½ cup quartered and thinly sliced
   red onion
1 large tomato, diced
1 medium sweet apple, diced
¼ cup thinly sliced fresh basil
2 tablespoons apple cider vinegar
1 tablespoon extra-virgin olive oil
Salt
Freshly ground black pepper

SUBSTITUTION TIP: I love apples in this recipe, but other fruit will work, too, like diced peaches or nectarines.

1. In a medium bowl, stir together the red onion, tomato, apple, and basil. Drizzle with apple cider vinegar and olive oil. Sprinkle with salt and black pepper.

2. Stir well. Taste and adjust the seasonings as desired.

CORN, TOMATO, AND CUCUMBER SALAD WITH DILL

SERVES 4

PREP TIME: 10 MINUTES

VEGAN

Fresh corn, tomato, and cucumbers combine with fragrant dill in this light, herby salad. It's a perfect counter to heavier pastas. Leftovers can be stored in an airtight container and should be eaten within 5 days.

2 ears corn, cooked and kernels cut from the cob (about 1 cup kernels)
1 large tomato, diced
1 medium cucumber, diced
2 tablespoons white wine vinegar or apple cider vinegar
1 tablespoon finely chopped fresh dill
1 tablespoon extra-virgin olive oil
Salt
Freshly ground black pepper

In a large bowl, combine the corn kernels, tomato, cucumber, white wine vinegar, dill, olive oil, salt, and black pepper. Stir well.

SUBSTITUTION TIP: Other light vinegars can be used in this recipe as well, like champagne vinegar or tarragon vinegar. Play with the flavors and find the one you love best.

CAPRESE SKEWERS

SERVES 4

PREP TIME: 10 MINUTES

VEGETARIAN

Simple but elegant, these skewers combine the familiar and beloved flavors of caprese salad in an easy handheld form. These are great for serving at dinner parties, but they are fun for enjoying at home with just the family, too.

16 cherry or grape tomatoes
16 leaves fresh basil
16 mozzarella balls (bocconcini or ciliegine)
Balsamic glaze
Extra-virgin olive oil
Salt
Freshly ground black pepper

SUBSTITUTION TIP: Fresh mozzarella cut into ¾-inch cubes can be substituted for the mozzarella balls.

On cocktail skewers (about 2 to 3 inches long, with decorative ends), thread a tomato, a basil leaf, and a mozzarella ball. Continue this process with the remaining skewers until all the ingredients have been used. Drizzle with the balsamic glaze and olive oil. Season with salt and black pepper.

PANZANELLA SALAD

SERVES 4

PREP TIME: 15 MINUTES

30 MINUTES, VEGETARIAN

Panzanella is a classic salad featuring torn pieces of old bread that sop up all the flavors. It's delightful. This version flavors the salad with robust balsamic vinegar and sharp blue cheese.

2 cups torn day-old Italian-style bread
1 cup halved grape or cherry tomatoes
½ cup thinly sliced and or finely chopped red onion
¼ to ½ cup crumbled blue cheese
3 tablespoons balsamic vinegar
2 tablespoons extra-virgin olive oil
Salt
Freshly ground black pepper

In a large bowl, combine the bread, tomatoes, onion, blue cheese, balsamic vinegar, and olive oil. Season with salt and black pepper. Toss well to combine. Cover and chill for 30 minutes before serving.

SUBSTITUTION TIP: For a Greek version of this salad, use feta cheese instead of blue cheese and add ½ cup kalamata olives to the recipe. Also, use white wine vinegar instead of balsamic.

EASY ROASTED ASPARAGUS
AND SHALLOTS

SERVES 4

PREP TIME: 10 MINUTES | COOK TIME: 15 MINUTES

30 MINUTES, VEGAN

Roasting does an amazing thing to vegetables—it brings out their earthier, sweeter, and more nuanced flavors. This simple recipe for asparagus is a crowd favorite. Be sure to use a large baking sheet so the asparagus and shallots have plenty of room to cook.

1 to 1½ pounds fresh asparagus, tough ends removed
1 shallot, halved and thickly sliced
1 tablespoon extra-virgin olive oil
Salt
Freshly ground black pepper

OPTION TIP: If you enjoy cheese, this side dish is lovely with a sprinkling of Parmesan, feta, or blue cheese. You can either add it at the end of the roasting time or top it when serving.

1. Preheat the oven to 400°F.

2. On a large baking sheet, arrange the asparagus and shallot in a single layer. Drizzle with the olive oil and sprinkle with salt and black pepper.

3. Roast for 10 to 12 minutes, or to the desired doneness.

SWEET AND SPICY STEAMED BROCCOLI

SERVES 4

PREP TIME: 5 MINUTES | COOK TIME: 15 MINUTES

30 MINUTES, QUICK PREP, VEGAN

Tender steamed broccoli is tossed with a sweet and spicy sauce in this easy recipe. This is excellent as a side dish and leftovers reheat well, too. Adjust the amount of sriracha depending on how much spiciness you like. A single teaspoon will make the sauce mild, while a tablespoon will give it more bite.

4 cups fresh broccoli florets
1 tablespoon rice vinegar
1 tablespoon soy sauce
1 tablespoon honey
2 teaspoons sriracha
1 teaspoon peeled and grated
  fresh ginger
1 garlic clove, minced

OPTION TIP: For a spicier version, use a tablespoon of sriracha.

1. In a large pot of boiling water with a steamer rack, steam the broccoli for 8 to 10 minutes, until crisp-tender. Transfer the broccoli to a medium bowl.

2. In a small bowl, whisk together the rice vinegar, soy sauce, honey, sriracha, ginger, and garlic. Toss with the broccoli. Let the broccoli sit for 5 minutes and toss again.

SESAME BRUSSELS SPROUTS

SERVES 4

PREP TIME: 15 MINUTES | COOK TIME: 25 MINUTES

VEGAN

Brussels sprouts have come a long way from being the butt of vegetable jokes, haven't they? Those who love them, or who haven't had them prepared well yet, will want to try this recipe. Tender Brussels sprouts are flavored with sesame and soy in this easy sautéed dish. As you are preparing them, be sure to trim any outer leaves that are less than perfect.

1 tablespoon extra-virgin olive oil
4 cups halved Brussels sprouts
1 tablespoon soy sauce
1 tablespoon sesame seeds
1 teaspoon sesame oil
Salt
Freshly ground black pepper

SUBSTITUTION TIP: This recipe can also be made with cauliflower. Cut the cauliflower into bite-size pieces before cooking.

1. In a large sauté pan or skillet, heat the olive oil over medium heat. Add the Brussels sprouts and sauté, stirring occasionally, until the Brussels sprouts are beginning to brown, 15 to 20 minutes.

2. Add the soy sauce, sesame seeds, and sesame oil to the sauté pan and toss vigorously. Remove the sauté pan from the heat. Taste and season with salt and black pepper, as desired.

ROASTED BEETS WITH FETA AND ONIONS

SERVES 6 TO 8

PREP TIME: 15 MINUTES | COOK TIME: 40 MINUTES

VEGETARIAN

Sweet beets and Vidalia onions combine with salty feta cheese in this easy roasted recipe ideal for beet lovers. If you have leftovers, store them in an airtight container and eat them within 5 days.

4 to 6 large beets, cubed (about 4 cups)
1 small Vidalia onion, cut into chunks
2 tablespoons extra-virgin olive oil
Salt
Freshly ground black pepper
¼ cup crumbled feta cheese

1. Preheat the oven to 400°F.

2. On a large baking sheet, arrange the beets and onion. Drizzle with the olive oil and season generously with salt and black pepper. Stir to coat the vegetables.

3. Roast for 20 minutes without disturbing. Stir. Roast for an additional 15 to 20 minutes, until the onion and beets are tender.

4. Remove the baking sheet from the oven and transfer the beets and onions to a serving bowl. Sprinkle with the feta cheese. Stir and serve.

INGREDIENT TIP: If you can't find large beets, choose baby beets and quarter them. Also, other crumbly cheeses can be substituted for the feta cheese in this recipe.

HERBED ROASTED CARROTS

SERVES 4

PREP TIME: 15 MINUTES | COOK TIME: 30 MINUTES

VEGAN

Sweet and soft on the inside and bursting with herbed flavor on the outside, these roasted carrots are a family favorite. If you happen to be using very thick carrots, be sure to halve or quarter them.

1 pound carrots, cut into 1-inch pieces
   (cut in half if thick)
2 tablespoons extra-virgin olive oil
1 teaspoon salt
½ teaspoon paprika
½ teaspoon dried thyme
½ teaspoon dried rosemary

INGREDIENT TIP: You want all the carrot pieces to be roughly the same size. This will ensure they cook evenly.

1. Preheat the oven to 400°F.

2. Spread the carrots out on a medium baking sheet. In a small bowl, stir together the olive oil, salt, paprika, thyme, and rosemary. Drizzle over the carrots. Stir to coat the carrots.

3. Roast for 15 minutes. Stir. Roast for an additional 10 to 15 minutes, stirring occasionally, until the carrots are tender.

SAUTÉED GREEN BEANS WITH GARLICKY BREAD CRUMBS

SERVES 4

PREP TIME: 10 MINUTES | COOK TIME: 15 MINUTES

30 MINUTES, VEGAN

When can green beans be more than a basic side dish? When you do something special with them. The combination of garlicky flavor and bread crumb texture make these green beans something very special. Be sure to cut the beans into similarly sized pieces for best results.

2 cups halved fresh green beans
¼ cup water
1 tablespoon extra-virgin olive oil
2 to 3 garlic cloves, minced
Salt
Freshly ground black pepper
1 tablespoon dried bread crumbs

TIME-SAVING TIP: Fresh green beans work best in this recipe, but steam-in-the-bag beans can be substituted. If using those, omit step 1 and add the cooked green beans to the pot in step 2.

1. In a large pot over medium heat, combine the green beans and water. Cover the pot and cook for 10 minutes. Drain any remaining water.

2. Add the olive oil and garlic to the pot. Stir well for 1 minute, until the garlic is fragrant. Season with salt and black pepper and dust with the bread crumbs. Stir well.

3. Remove the pot from the heat and serve.

GARLIC-PARSLEY ROASTED CAULIFLOWER

SERVES 4

PREP TIME: 10 MINUTES | COOK TIME: 30 MINUTES

VEGAN

Roasted cauliflower is one of my dinner table staples. In this recipe, cauliflower is mixed with olive oil, garlic, salt, and sugar before being baked to golden, tender perfection. Then it's tossed with fresh parsley just before serving for a delightful and flavorful side.

1 medium head cauliflower, broken into 1-inch florets
2 tablespoons extra-virgin olive oil
4 garlic cloves, minced
1 teaspoon salt
⅛ teaspoon sugar
Freshly ground black pepper
2 tablespoons minced fresh parsley

1. Preheat the oven to 400°F.

2. On a medium nonstick baking sheet, arrange the cauliflower florets in a single layer. Drizzle with the olive oil and then sprinkle with the garlic, salt, sugar, and black pepper. Stir to combine.

3. Roast for 20 minutes. Stir. Roast for an additional 10 to 15 minutes, until the cauliflower is golden in places.

4. Remove the baking sheet from the oven. Sprinkle the cauliflower with the parsley and toss to combine.

MAKE IT EASIER TIP: Fresh cauliflower florets can be used in place of cutting them from a head of cauliflower. You'll need about 4 to 5 cups of cauliflower florets for this recipe.

BROWN SUGAR CORNBREAD

SERVES 6 TO 8

PREP TIME: 10 MINUTES | COOK TIME: 25 MINUTES

VEGETARIAN

Soft and not too sweet, this easy cornbread recipe is excellent for enjoying with spicy pastas and other saucy meals. It's excellent served with the Sloppy Joe Penne (page 47) or the Black Bean and Veggie Enchilada Rotini (page 32).

Nonstick cooking spray
1 cup yellow cornmeal
1 cup all-purpose flour
1 tablespoon baking powder
1 teaspoon salt
1 cup milk
½ cup packed light brown sugar
2 large eggs, lightly beaten
¼ cup unsalted butter, melted and
   cooled slightly

1. Preheat the oven to 400°F.

2. Spray an 8-by-8-inch baking pan with nonstick cooking spray and set aside.

3. In a large bowl, sift together the cornmeal, flour, baking powder, and salt.

4. Make a well in the center of the cornmeal mixture and add the milk, brown sugar, eggs, and butter. Stir to combine.

5. Pour the batter into the prepared baking pan and tilt to distribute evenly.

6. Bake for 20 to 25 minutes, until the cornbread is golden and a toothpick inserted in the center comes out clean.

OPTION TIP: For a heartier cornbread, add ½ cup corn kernels to the batter before pouring it into the baking pan.

GARLIC BREAD

SERVES 4

PREP TIME: 15 MINUTES | COOK TIME: 15 MINUTES

30 MINUTES, VEGETARIAN

Forget the store-bought garlic bread with the grainy texture to the butter. Making garlic bread from scratch at home is easy, economical, and more flavorful.

1 loaf Italian bread, sliced in half lengthwise
½ cup (1 stick) unsalted butter, room temperature
½ teaspoon salt
3 garlic cloves, minced
½ teaspoon dried basil

INGREDIENT TIP: The softer the butter, the better. Be sure to mash the butter mixture well to evenly distribute all the ingredients.

1. Preheat the oven to 375°F.

2. Line a medium baking sheet with aluminum foil or parchment paper and place the halves of the bread on it with the cut sides facing up. Set aside.

3. In a small bowl, mash together the butter, salt, garlic, and basil until fully combined. Spread half of this mixture on each half of the loaf.

4. Bake for 10 to 13 minutes, until the butter is fully melted. Slice and serve.

CHEESY ARTICHOKE BREAD

SERVES 6

PREP TIME: 15 MINUTES | COOK TIME: 20 MINUTES

VEGETARIAN

When can a bread recipe act like an appetizer? When it's a robust loaf like this. This one is filling—Italian bread is topped with a seasoned butter that has Romano cheese mixed in and then topped with chopped artichoke hearts and mozzarella. Once it's done baking, this fabulous side dish is a joy to eat.

1 loaf Italian bread, sliced in half lengthwise

½ cup (1 stick) unsalted butter, room temperature

½ teaspoon salt

½ teaspoon dried thyme

¼ cup freshly grated Romano cheese

1 cup coarsely chopped frozen or canned artichoke hearts

1 cup shredded mozzarella cheese

1. Preheat the oven to 375°F.

2. Line a medium baking sheet with aluminum foil or parchment paper and place the halves of the bread on it with the cut sides facing up. Set aside.

3. In a small bowl, mash together the butter, salt, thyme, and Romano cheese. Spread this mixture evenly on the two loaf halves. Top each with half the artichoke hearts and half the mozzarella cheese.

4. Bake for 14 to 16 minutes, until the bread is beginning to brown at the edges. Remove the baking sheet from the oven and allow the bread to cool for 5 minutes before slicing and serving.

SUBSTITUTION TIP: No Romano cheese? Other hard cheeses like Parmesan and Asiago can be substituted.

The Dirty Dozen and the Clean Fifteen™

A nonprofit environmental watchdog organization called Environmental Working Group (EWG) looks at data supplied by the US Department of Agriculture (USDA) and the Food and Drug Administration (FDA) about pesticide residues. Each year it compiles a list of the best and worst pesticide loads found in commercial crops. You can use these lists to decide which fruits and vegetables to buy organic to minimize your exposure to pesticides and which produce is considered safe enough to buy conventionally. This does not mean they are pesticide-free, though, so wash these fruits and vegetables thoroughly.

Dirty Dozen™

- apples
- celery
- cherries
- grapes
- nectarines
- peaches
- pears
- potatoes
- spinach
- strawberries
- sweet bell peppers
- tomatoes

*Additionally, nearly three-quarters of hot pepper samples contained pesticide residues

Clean Fifteen™

- asparagus
- avocados
- broccoli
- cabbages
- cantaloupes
- cauliflower
- eggplants
- honeydew melons
- kiwis
- mangoes
- onions
- papayas
- pineapples
- sweet corn
- sweet peas (frozen)

Measurement Conversions

VOLUME EQUIVALENTS (Liquid)

US Standard	US Standard (ounces)	Metric (approximate)
2 tablespoons	1 fl. oz.	30 mL
¼ cup	2 fl. oz.	60 mL
½ cup	4 fl. oz.	120 mL
1 cup	8 fl. oz.	240 mL
1½ cups	12 fl. oz	355 mL
2 cups or 1 pint	16 fl. oz.	475 mL
4 cups or 1 quart	32 fl. oz.	1 L
1 gallon	128 fl. oz.	4 L

OVEN TEMPERATURES

Fahrenheit (F)	Celsius (C) (approximate)
250°F	120°C
300°F	150°C
325°F	165°C
350°F	180°C
375°F	190°C
400°F	200°C
425°F	220°C
450°F	230°C

VOLUME EQUIVALENTS (Dry)

US Standard	Metric (approximate)
⅛ teaspoon	0.5 mL
¼ teaspoon	1 mL
½ teaspoon	2 mL
¾ teaspoon	4 mL
1 teaspoon	5 mL
1 tablespoon	15 mL
¼ cup	59 mL
⅓ cup	79 mL
½ cup	118 mL
⅔ cup	156 mL
¾ cup	177 mL
1 cup	235 mL
2 cups or 1 pint	475 mL
3 cups	700 mL
4 cups or 1 quart	1 L

WEIGHT EQUIVALENTS

US Standard	Metric (approximate)
½ ounce	15 g
1 ounce	30 g
2 ounces	60 g
4 ounces	115 g
8 ounces	225 g
12 ounces	340 g
16 ounces or 1 pound	455 g

Recipe Index

Index

Acknowledgments

What do you do when you are working on so many pasta recipes at once that you can't possibly eat them all? You store them for take-to-school lunches. And that's precisely what my kids and I did. No waste!

Related: No more freezer space!

Writing a cookbook requires a lot—not just from the cookbook author who develops, tests, and retests recipes, but also from those who help with the process by lending their taste buds and palates. To that end, I have to thank my children, Will and Paige, as well as Gibran Graham, for eating so many of these recipes. Often for the same meal. You all are the best tasters a girl could ask for.

A very special thank you to Paige, especially, who acted as my sous chef for many of these recipes. I am so proud of your knife skills and appreciate every bit of chopping and mincing you did to help me create and test these recipes.

Thank you also to my parents and siblings, Susan, Rick, Zach, and Haley, for your continuing support of all my kitchen endeavors. I can't wait to cook for you again.

To my readers of *Sarah's Cucina Bella*, old and new, thank you so much for all your support and kindness over the years. Your readership means the world to me.

Thank you to Marthine Satris, Elizabeth Castoria, and Kim Suarez, all of Callisto Media, for selecting me for this book and ushering me through the process so seamlessly.

And finally, thanks to my late grandmother, Betty Wilson Walker, who taught me to appreciate a well-crafted pasta with each and every bowl of her lovingly made spaghetti and homemade sauce. I'll never stop missing you.

About the Author

Credit: Gabor Degre / Bangor Daily News

Sarah Walker Caron is an award-winning food columnist and writer whose work has appeared in *Fine Cooking*, *BELLA Magazine*, and *Yum for Kids*, as well as on BettyCrocker.com, the *TODAY Show* website, SheKnows.com, and more. She is the author of *The Super Easy 5-Ingredient Cookbook*, and coauthor of *Grains as Mains: Modern Recipes Using Ancient Grains*. She writes a monthly cooking column for *Bangor Metro* magazine. She was named the 2015 Maine local columnist of the year by the Maine Press Association. Her food blog, *Sarah's Cucina Bella* (SarahsCucinaBella.com), has been delighting readers with a unique blend of life and food writing since it was founded in 2005. Sarah is a graduate of Barnard College and lives in Maine with her two kids.

CPSIA information can be obtained
at www.ICGtesting.com
Printed in the USA
BVHW021326201218
535992BV00022B/285/P